20 M

19 M

Turnpike

19 M

Hutton Turnpike

20 M

21 M

Parsonage

Hutton Hall

D Booth Esq

Hutton

Ilfords

Ingrave

Firth

Brick House

Ingrave Hall Wood

Brick Kiln Farm

Ingrave Hall

Auga
Spring

Parsonage

Nutt Grove

Charvill

Sealings

Heron Lodg

Ingrave

Heron H

Marshs
Hopkins

Thorndon
Hall
Lord Petre

Heron Gate

ilderditch

Common

Little

BRENTWOOD
A HISTORY

2004

Published by
PHILLIMORE & CO. LTD
Shopwyke Manor Barn, Chichester, West Sussex, England

ISBN 1 86077 279 X

Printed and bound in Great Britain by
CROMWELL PRESS
Trowbridge, Wiltshire

Contents

Preface and Acknowledgements

A few years ago, a furore broke out in Brentwood when it was alleged that the town had no history. The allegation was quickly rebutted from all sides. Brentwood's history is typical of that of many places which started as small towns with a church, market and fair, and experienced their greatest period of growth in the 19th and 20th centuries. Yet Brentwood, unlike many other towns, has a good claim to a place in national history since it was at a court held in the town in 1381 that the Peasants' Revolt got under way. The experiences of the townspeople who settled in the town and ensured its growth and prosperity make Brentwood's history come alive. In the past 200 years especially they stand out as individuals, and their contributions to the town are still felt at the present day. Men like Cornelius Butler, Frank Landon, John Larkin and J.J. Crowe made a lasting impact on Brentwood. John Larkin's *Fireside Talks about Brentwood* and *More Fireside Talks* provide vivid detail as to what the town was like in the later 19th and early 20th century.

Sums of money have been given in their historical form, as they were before decimalisation. The pound was made up of 20 shillings, and each shilling of 12 pence. The shilling corresponds to a face value of five new pence, and the pound to 100 new pence. No attempt has been made to estimate the present-day value of the sums of money cited in the text, since inflation and changing circumstances make this virtually impossible.

In writing this history, I have incurred a number of debts, and would like to thank Doreen Acton, Paul Billett, John Copeland, Philip Povey and John Ward for advice and information. Any remaining mistakes are mine. I would like to thank the following people for illustrations: Doreen Acton for nos 121-3; Michael Beale for no. 84; John Copeland for nos 124, 127, 132-4; Philip Povey for nos 27, 51, 60, 70, 86, 103, 107, 141, 143 and 144; and John Ward for the endpapers, 1, 28, 33 and 52.

The book is dedicated to the memory of my mother, Gladys Amy Ward, who spent the greater part of her life in Brentwood, and did much research on the history of the town. Through her writings and lectures, and as a founder-member and long-term secretary of the Brentwood and District Historical Society, she encouraged local history in Brentwood, and instilled in many people a strong interest in the past.

window. The east window was rebuilt in brick in the 16th century, and took up a large part of the wall above the altar. During the Middle Ages, there was also an altar on the south side of the nave which was lit by Perpendicular-style windows. After the Reformation, the west window was blocked up, and galleries were erected on three sides of the nave. The floor was paved, but this was boarded over when the building became a school.

Within a few years of its foundation the chapel became the centre of a political storm when a disgraced royal minister was arrested there. Hubert de Burgh had been Henry III's justiciar, or chief minister, but he was sacked in 1232, forced to surrender his castles and offices, and ordered to appear before the barons of the realm to render account of the royal revenues which had passed through his hands. He fled from court, but was pursued by the king's men and took refuge in a chapel which, according the the Annals of Dunstable, was at *Boisars*. His pursuers dragged him out of the chapel, and, according to one story, summoned a blacksmith to put fetters on him. The blacksmith refused, since he regarded Hubert as the saviour of the realm during the civil war about fifteen years before, and the king's men took Hubert back with them to the Tower of London. In response to the bishop of London's protest at the violation of sanctuary, Hubert was brought back to the chapel, but the sheriff of Essex was ordered to besiege it and not let Hubert escape. Hubert eventually surrendered.

There was another link between the chapel and the royal court much later on. In 1393, a chantry was established there by Edmund of Langley, Duke of York, to celebrate daily Masses for the salvation of the soul of his sister Isabella, Countess of Bedford, daughter of Edward III, who had died in 1379. Prayers were also to be said for her youngest brother, Thomas, Duke of Gloucester, and for the king and queen. The foundation of chantries to pray for the living and the dead was common at the time, but it is not known why Brentwood

4 *The west front of St Thomas's chapel about 1856.*

chapel was chosen. Possibly this was due to its dedication to St Thomas of Canterbury, or possibly to its location on the main road from London to Colchester.

Whatever the significance of the chapel to the elite, it provided an important focus for the townspeople, who were always anxious to ensure its continued existence. In 1373, the inhabitants complained to Simon Sudbury, Bishop of London, that the abbot of St Osyth was failing to maintain the chapel and had leased the chaplain's house to laymen. The abbot promised that in future he would pay 50 shillings a year for the support of the chaplain; at the same time he asserted that the chaplain's house had not been let. Over sixty years later, in 1440, the men of Brentwood appealed to Pope Eugenius IV, pointing out that the parish church of South Weald was very remote from Brentwood, and that in time of floods and bad weather Brentwood children died on their way to baptism, and the inhabitants were left without Mass and the sacraments of the Church. It was usual at that time for babies to be baptised when only a few days old. The pope ordered the abbot of St Osyth to investigate the situation, and, if the allegations were true, to allow the chaplain to conduct baptisms and celebrate Mass in the chapel. This, however, was only to happen when the weather was so bad that it was impossible to get to the parish church. Later events show that Brentwood people continued to regard their chapel as essential to the well-being of the town.

5 *The chapel ruins in 1959.*

6 *A.B. Bamford's depiction in 1892 of the 15 ft entrance from the High Street into Crown Street and the former market-place. The election riot of 1874 took place in front of Carter's shop. The shop was demolished when Crown Street was widened.*

7 *The former market-place and Crown Street as depicted by A.B. Bamford in 1892, looking towards the High Street. The building on the left is the rear of the King's Head inn which probably dated from the 15th century. It was demolished about 1970.*

Brentwood's position on the main road made it a convenient centre for local administration. Law and custom were enforced at the manorial court of Costed, held by the officials of the abbot of St Osyth, and at the county and hundred courts, the hundred being a subdivision of the county. Brentwood was close to the boundary of the hundreds of Barstable and Chafford, and in the late 14th century courts were held in the town for both hundreds. The most notorious session was held on 30 May 1381, when the Justice of the Peace John Bampton investigated the non-payment of the third poll tax which had been widely evaded all over England. Three villages in Barstable hundred – Fobbing, Corringham and Stanford-le-Hope – refused to give him another penny. They tried to put John and his officers to death, but he fled to London and the common people took to the woods and stirred up revolt. Shortly afterwards, on 2 June, Sir Robert Belknapp, Chief Justice of the Court of Common Pleas, came to Brentwood to punish them. He was told that he was a traitor to king and kingdom, and was forced to swear on the Bible that he would never again hold a similar session. He departed home at speed. By then, the Peasants' Revolt was under way in Kent and Essex.

8   *The courtyard of the* White Hart *as depicted by A.B. Bamford in 1892, showing the gallery which gave access to the rooms on the first floor.*

9 *The courtyard of the* White Hart *about 1960.*

The main road was of vital importance to the market, which was frequented by men and women from the nearby villages. The men of Hutton brought their produce for sale in Brentwood market in the later 14th century, after the Black Death, instead of taking it to Battle Abbey in Sussex which held the lordship of Hutton. A variety of trades was practised in the town. The taxation return for 1327 for South Weald and Brentwood refers to John le Tannere, Henry le Waterladere, Walter le Coupere, Stephen le Skinnere, Stephen le Bakere, and Sewal and Richard le Cok. A dyer, draper and spicer are mentioned in the mid-15th century.

As well as catering for local needs, the market supplied food for London. London merchants found towns on main roads, such as Romford, Brentwood and Chelmsford, particularly convenient for securing the City's food supplies, and several are found at Brentwood in the late Middle Ages, doing business and acquiring property. Brentwood men were also doing business in London. In 1419, John Stacy of Brentwood owed money to Richard Justice of London, armourer, and in 1466 John Weskam alias Gardyner of Brentwood handed over all his goods to Thomas Atherwas, a London merchant, in payment of his debt of £13 6s. 8d. Nicholas Martyn, spurrier, and Robert Merston, salter, both of London, acquired shops and land in Brentwood in the early 15th century, while Robert Lynge, a London ironmonger, was making similar

10   *The* Golden Fleece *inn, Brook Street, from A.B. Bamford's print of 1892.*

purchases in the 1520s and 1530s. At least one London merchant acquired a country estate in the Brentwood area in the early 15th century, when the Welshman and vintner, Lewis John, built Old Thorndon Hall.

Merchants, travellers and pilgrims passing through Brentwood brought business to the inns. Not all were lucky when they were in the town. Thomas Neulond lost his wallet with his business receipts when attacked by 'certain evil disposed persons' at Brentwood. When the new Woolworths was being built in 1968 (now Marks and Spencer), a hoard of 308 silver coins was discovered. The coins date from the 14th and early 15th centuries, and the hoard was deposited about 1420. The face value of the hoard amounted to £3 1s. 7d., and it is likely that the money was buried with the intention of recovering it later.

A number of 15th-century houses and inns survive. All are timber-framed buildings. The *White Hart* dates partly from the early 15th century, and partly from the first half of the 16th, and it is likely that both merchants and pilgrims lodged there. It was built on an L-shaped plan. The hall in front would have been the principal room for eating, drinking and doing

11 *The 15th-century house at 60-64 High Street. The photograph was taken in the 1960s, showing the building divided into three shops. The house can still be seen.*

business, while in the wing there were chambers overlooking the courtyard, those on the first floor being entered from a gallery; the gallery has been altered in modern times but can still be traced. There may have been an earlier inn on the site, as 13th-century pottery has been found in the courtyard. The *Golden Fleece* in Brook Street contains work dating from the late 13th to the mid-16th centuries. It was an inn by 1745, but its earlier use is uncertain. Numbers 60-64 and 63-65 High Street also date from the 15th century; numbers 63-65 were restored in 1974.

12 *A view of the rear of 60-64 High Street, taken from South Street.*

13 *63-65 High Street. The house was built in the 15th century, and the photograph was taken before the restoration of 1974.*

Brentwood at the end of the Middle Ages was a small but busy town, frequented by pilgrims, merchants and people from the surrounding villages. Migrants from elsewhere in England settled in the town, and a document of 1394 mentions an Irish labourer, William Whyte. Brentwood was in no sense an isolated community, cut off from the rest of the British Isles. Men and women made use of the royal courts at Westminster, just as they used the manor court and Quarter Sessions. In 1468, Joan Nightingale, probably a widow, was thought by her neighbours to be a leper; leprosy was a dreaded disease in the medieval world. She was ordered by the king to be examined, and, if leprous, to be removed to a solitary place. Joan, however, appealed to the Chancellor, the Crown's highest official, was examined by the royal physicians, and declared free of the disease. No more is known about her, but it is to be hoped that she ended her life in peace.

TWO

The Sixteenth Century: Continuity and Change

The reigns of the Tudor monarchs witnessed great social, political and religious change in England. Henry VIII's Reformation of the 1530s saw an end to the Pope's authority, and the Dissolution of the Monasteries. Protestant forms of religious worship were established under Edward VI and Elizabeth (1547-53, and 1558-1603), although there was a short return to Roman Catholicism under Mary in the mid-1550s. At the same time, new families, who often made their fortunes as merchants, lawyers or high officials at court, became members of the gentry and nobility. All these developments had an impact on the localities, and matters which had been taken for granted for centuries were subject to sudden change.

14 *The east front of Weald Hall, as depicted by A.B. Bamford in 1892, showing the Tudor house built by Sir Antony Browne. The Hall was demolished after the Second World War.*

Since the 11th and 12th centuries South Weald and Brentwood had been part of the lordships of Waltham Abbey and the abbey of St Osyth. St Osyth's was dissolved in 1539, and Waltham in 1540, the last English monastery to be suppressed. All their lands and possessions came into the king's hands. Ambitious officials were eager to buy the estates, and a place like Brentwood was near enough to London for them to maintain their connections with the court. Sir William Petre, the king's Secretary, purchased Ingatestone, and the Thorndon estate was acquired by his son John in 1573. South Weald was granted to the Tuke family, and subsequently sold to the king's Chancellor, Richard Lord Rich, and then, in 1548, to Sir Antony Browne who became Chief Justice of the Court of Common Pleas and established his seat at Weald Hall. The manor of Costed, including the town of Brentwood, likewise passed through a number of hands, being held by Henry VIII's chief minister, Thomas Cromwell before his execution in 1540, and by his divorced wife Anne of Cleves between 1541 and 1557. It then came into the hands of Antony Browne, and after his death in 1567 the Browne family continued to hold it for just over a hundred years.

Tudor courtiers and lawyers set a high value on education, and were largely responsible for establishing grammar schools in Essex. Antony Browne, supported by local people, founded the Grammar School at Brentwood on 28 July 1558. He and his heirs were named patrons of the School, with the right to appoint the schoolmaster for life and two local men as wardens of the

15 *A view of 1904, showing the north front of Weald Hall which was refaced in the 18th century.*

16 *Brentwood School, from the print by A.B. Bamford, 1892. The Old Big Schoolroom behind the Old Elm Tree was a one-storey building until 1854.*

school's lands during their pleasure. The schoolmaster was to be in holy orders, and this remained the case down to the 19th century. The first schoolmaster was George Otway, described as 'a worthy man and sound in religion'. To start with, the school was held in the chapel and house of Redcross, on the corner of London Road and Honeypot Lane, which had been built by the London ironmonger John Andrew (d.1519) and used as a school towards the end of his life. The Old Big Schoolroom in Ingrave Road was built by Sir Antony's stepdaughter Dorothy and her husband Edmund Huddleston in 1568, and the school was held there down to the 19th century.

Education at the Grammar School was based on Latin and the classics. A knowledge of the classics was regarded as the hallmark of the educated man, and Latin was still used across Europe for works of learning. John Greenwood, who succeeded Otway as schoolmaster in 1570, published *Syntaxis et Prosodia* twenty years later, and the book was presumably used in the school. The *Syntaxis* provided the pupil with the rules of Latin grammar; Greenwood wrote in verse and gave examples from a wide range of Latin poets. The *Prosodia* gave the rules for writing Latin verse.

17 *The* Swan *inn as depicted by A.B. Bamford in 1892.*

The boys had to be able to read and write before entering the school, and the Statutes of 1622 throw light on their school life. A free education was given to the boys of South Weald parish and of any parish within three miles of the school. School hours during the winter were from 7-11 a.m. and 1-5p.m., and in summer school started one hour earlier and finished one hour later. The boys had about three weeks holiday at Christmas, about ten days at Easter, and about ten days at Pentecost. The school-day began and ended with prayers, and the scholars attended service at St Thomas's chapel on Wednesday and Friday mornings, and at their parish church on Sundays. Discipline was strict, and regular attendance was expected. Boys who were found to be disobedient, or were drunkards, dicers or swearers were expelled.

As far as the 16th-century religious changes were concerned, Brentwood people took a cautious line and most accepted the new laws ordained by Henry VIII and Edward VI, although four men and one woman were found guilty of heresy in 1546 at a court held at Brentwood. The return to Roman Catholicism under Mary, however, provoked considerable protest in Essex, and many who refused to recant their Protestant views were burnt at the stake. At Brentwood, William Hunter suffered this fate at the age of nineteen. According to the account written by his brother Robert, William was apprenticed to a silk weaver in London, but was dismissed when he refused to receive communion at Easter Mass. William came home to Brentwood, and one day was found in the chapel reading the Bible; Henry VIII had authorised the placing of the English Bible in churches in 1538, but under Mary reading the Bible was regarded as a sign of heresy. William was examined by the vicar of South Weald and accused of denying the doctrine of transubstantiation which laid down that the bread and wine became the Body and Blood of Christ when consecrated by the priest during Mass. Sir Antony Browne sent William to Edmund Bonner, Bishop of London for further questioning. Bonner kept him in prison for nine months and urged him to recant, finally offering to set him up in business in London if he renounced heresy. William refused, and in March 1555 was brought back to Brentwood, lodging at the *Swan* inn and visited by his parents and others. He was burnt to death at the town's end where the archery butts stood, and Antony Browne was present. Traditionally, an elm tree marked the site of his death, very close to where the Schoolroom was to be built 13 years later. The elm was still there, though dead, in the mid-20th century. In 1861 a monument to William Hunter was erected in Shenfield Road.

Most Brentwood people accepted the Reformation, but they were ready to fight for their chapel, which continued to be a focal point of the community. Some Brentwood people left bequests to the chapel, such as the innholder Thomas Williams who bequeathed £10 towards the support of divine service there in 1585, and also left £5 for the poor. Antony Browne's great-nephew and successor, Wistan Browne, made it clear in 1577 that he wanted to close the chapel. He regarded it as his private possession and probably wished to save money. When Antony Browne purchased Costed manor, part of the

18   *The memorial to William Hunter erected in Shenfield Road in 1861.*

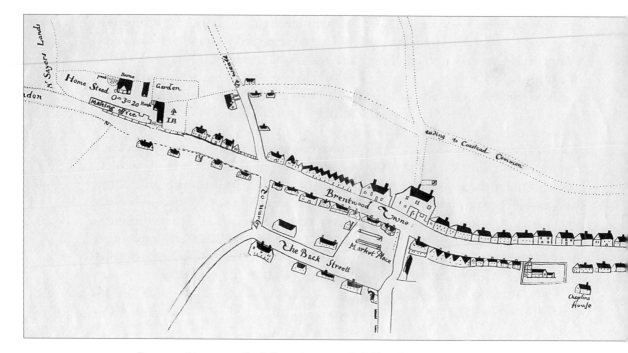

19 *Brentwood in 1717. Back Street is now called Hart Street. Kings Road and Weald Road were known as Warley Lane and Weald Lane in 1717. Crown Street was known as Webbs Lane or Love Lane. The* White Hart *was the largest building in the High Street.*

purchase price was remitted when he agreed that he and his successors would pay £5 a year to the chaplain. On 2 August 1577, Wistan Browne removed the pews from the chapel, and also the pulpit, great bell and the clock. Three days later, a riot broke out in the High Street when 30 women, led by Thomasine Tyler, surrounded the chapel. They were armed with what lay to hand at home, and their weapons included two hot spits, a hatchet, a great hammer, two kettles of hot water and a large sharp stone. They pulled the schoolmaster, Richard Brooke, out of the chapel and beat him, and then barricaded themselves inside. It was Wistan Browne's responsibility as sheriff of Essex to suppress the riot. He arrived at the chapel with two justices of the peace, but failed to arrest 17 of the women; one man refused to assist the justices, and another tried to rescue Thomasine Tyler when she was taken off to prison.

Elizabeth I's government was always perturbed by disorder, but they wanted to know the facts of the case before apportioning blame. Two days after the riot, Wistan Browne was summoned to appear before her Privy Council on 11 August, and in the meantime ordered to stop pulling down the chapel. The women who had been arrested were freed on bail. In a letter to the Essex justices of the peace on 21 September, the Privy Council set out its views. They considered that Wistan Browne was the 'chiefest cause' of the disorder, since he had stopped the inhabitants from using the chapel. The women rioters were due to be punished at the next Quarter Sessions, but the Privy Council wanted them to be fined only a small amount; they were to be proceeded against 'only for form's sake'. In due course, each woman was fined four pence, and each man two shillings, and the chapel remained open for the people of Brentwood.

The Browne family made a further attempt to close the chapel in the early 17th century. Four Brentwood townsmen brought a case against Sir Antony Browne III in the Court of the Exchequer in 1616. Like their predecessors, they pointed to the town's distance from South Weald church, and they emphasised the importance of Brentwood as a market town. There were 400 communicants in the town, many of them too old and weak to travel to South Weald. They alleged that Sir Antony had ceased to pay the £5 due to the chaplain, and refused to appoint one, on the grounds that the chapel was not a public place of worship. The Court found for the inhabitants. Sir Antony was ordered to appoint a chaplain, to make appointments in future, and to bear half the cost of repairs to the chapel and the chaplain's house. The rest of the cost was to be borne by the townspeople.

As stated by the inhabitants in 1616, Brentwood continued to be a thriving commercial centre, with numerous crafts and trades. The population grew during the 16th century. The subsidy return of 1524 points to a population of about 500, and it is likely that there was growth during the Elizabethan period, followed by stabilisation in the 17th century. The returns for the Hearth Tax of 1671 indicate that the population then was just short of 600. These figures are approximate; there was no national census until 1801. Under the Tudors, shops and houses were newly built or extended, and it is likely that the Elizabethan town was very similar to that depicted on the map of 1717. Houses clustered along the High Street. There were a few houses along London and Shenfield Roads, but little building along Ingrave Road apart from the Grammar School. A few houses existed round the market-place and in Back Street, but excavation in 2000 on a site bounded by Hart Street (Back Street) and Kings Road revealed that settlement was sparse from the Middle Ages until the 19th century. Three houses or shops were found, two of them showing evidence of medieval building, and the third with several large pits dating from the medieval period and later. Two probable ovens were discovered, and several post-medieval pits may indicate a tanning business.

A major addition to the High Street came with the building of the Assize House in 1579 for the holding of Quarter Sessions and the Crown Assizes. Brentwood was still the meeting-place for the hundreds of Barstable and Chafford, and also of Becontree. The Assize House was near the 'flesh shambles', and the site was later occupied by the Town Hall. The land was purchased by John Tyler, husband of Thomasine, and John Haukin at the request of the inhabitants, and it was subsequently quitclaimed to a trust of 25 men who were to build and maintain the Assize House. The building was impressive, timber-framed, with three gables and magnificently carved bargeboards which have been dated to about 1610. Some courts continued to be held at the Assize House in the 17th century, but increasingly they were held at Chelmsford. In 1712 the Assize House was described as 'ruinous', but it was repaired to house the justices at a cost of £53 6s. 4d. Soon afterwards, however, it was divided into three shops, and in 1830 the two tenants were the blacksmith Robert Harris and the butcher John Offin.

The market continued to flourish in Elizabethan times. In 1599, Will Kemp took on and won a bet to dance all the way from London to Norwich. He danced for nine days out of the three weeks it took him for the journey. As he passed through Brentwood the market-day crowds brought him to a standstill. Two cut-purses were arrested and claimed to belong to his party. Kemp denied knowledge of them, and they were put in the town gaol.

More is known of the Elizabethan than of the medieval people of Brentwood because of the greater survival of wills which throw light on occupations and lifestyle. The more prosperous members of the community invested in land and urban property; rents provided extra income and were a safeguard during old age or widowhood. Some men engaged in more than one occupation, such as John Darbye the elder who according to his will of 1560 was both blacksmith and brewer and also had farmland. William Cocke had a stall for selling cloth in Chelmsford market, and John Corrall, who was probably a butcher, had a stall in Brentwood market and another at Horndon-on-the-Hill. Certain men stand out as being frequently called on to act as executors of wills, notably the baker John Cocke. He looked after the goods of Agnes Brockas until the marriage of her niece and heiress, who was also John's god-daughter, and he was the executor of John Mosse in 1575, and of Richard Allcocke in 1580. In 1584, at the death-bed of Henry Pickering, he asked him what to do with his goods, and Henry replied that his wife Anne was to have them all. John received a bequest of a grey gown from Thomas Williams, innholder. He died in 1598, leaving a son and two daughters. He was not a prosperous man, as his land was to be sold to pay his debts, with any money over going to his daughters. All that he left to his wife was the household stuff that she brought to their marriage.

Levels of prosperity differed markedly, although on the whole standards of living rose in Elizabethan Essex. The more prosperous townsmen had plenty of household furnishings, and houses often had more rooms than in the Middle Ages, allowing greater privacy. The blacksmith, William Danwood alias Beane, referred to his hall, chamber and parlour in 1582, and his furnishings included six pewter saucers, six porringers, four pewter dishes, a latten basin and two brass pots. The main concern of the testators was focused

20 *The Assize House, built in 1579, and divided into shops in the 18th century. It was demolished about 1860 and replaced by the Town Hall in 1864.*

on their families and the desire to provide for the future well-being of widows and children. Christian Lucas in 1579 made special arrangements to finance the upbringing of her daughter's children. James and Michael Ingram were left in the care of William Welles, brewer, and Roger Holt, shoemaker, until the age of fourteen when they would probably have been apprenticed. Their brother John was to be in William's and Roger's care until he was twenty years old. The boys' mother was still alive, but she appears to have lacked financial resources.

Brentwood in the 16th century saw both continuity and change. There was continuity in the sense that shopkeeping and marketing were carried on along the same lines as in the medieval town. At the same time, there was substantial change. The destruction of Thomas Becket's shrine at Canterbury in 1538 put an end to pilgrimage. Services in the chapel came to be conducted according to the new Book of Common Prayer. The monastic lords disappeared, to be replaced by courtiers and lawyers who sought to close the chapel, but also initiated constructive developments. The Grammar School ensured an education for local boys, while the women's riot in 1577 and the building of the Assize House two years later displayed the strong sense of community in the town.

THREE

Local Government
and the Poor

The Tudor monarchs made the parish responsible for local government, under the supervision of the Justices of the Peace and Quarter Sessions, and the Vestry meeting constituted the hub of local government from the 16th down to the 19th centuries. In particular, the parish was expected to look after its roads and its poor, appointing surveyors of the highways and overseers of the poor along with the churchwardens. Brentwood was in a somewhat anomalous position as part of the parish of South Weald, and the recommendation in 1650 that Brentwood chapel should become a parish church was not implemented. However, from the late Middle Ages, Brentwood had a certain amount of autonomy through the operation of the court leet of the manor of Costed, and by the later 17th century the chapel Vestry was largely in control of town government, although still subject to South Weald in religious matters.

The court leet was held by the abbey of St Osyth down to the Dissolution to enforce law and order in Costed manor and to regulate local trade, and the courts continued after 1539 until 1831. The court appointed two constables every year to ensure that the peace was kept, two aleconners and two leathersealers to supervise brewing and the leather trade, and, in the 16th and 17th centuries, two inspectors of meat and fish to safeguard quality and hygiene in the food trade. The Vestry took over the nomination of the constables, aleconners and leathersealers in the late 17th century, although appointments officially continued to be made by the court leet. The Vestry elected a churchwarden (for South Weald) and a chapelwarden, overseers of the poor and surveyors of the highways, and a sidesman and beadle. All the offices were honorary, although a paid assistant overseer was appointed in 1832. The manor had its Cage, Pound and Stocks, the Cage and Pound being at the east end of the High Street in 1788. The Vestry met as needed, usually once a month in the later 18th century, although meetings were often less frequent earlier. Attendance was usually small.

Many of the men who held office in the town in the late 18th century were shopkeepers and tradesmen. Thus, in 1784, the victualler George Finch was chapelwarden, the maltster James Finch one of the four overseers of the poor, and the tallowchandler Thomas Davis one of the two aleconners. James Finch was proprietor of the *Robin Hood* on Gallows Green, the waste land between the Ongar and Doddinghurst Roads, although his tenant actually ran the victualling house. In 1789, George Finch was churchwarden, and the butcher John Offin chapelwarden; Thomas Wickwar, overseer, was a shoemaker, and Edward Finch, John Laurie and Charles Millington, three of the four constables, were a baker, linendraper, and carpenter respectively. John Offin owned several properties along the High Street.

According to the Elizabethan Poor Law, parishes were responsible for looking after poor inhabitants who were unable to support themselves, and they were allowed to levy rates in order to do this. Many of the poor were old or disabled people and orphaned children. No parish wished to take responsibility for outsiders, and, according to the law of settlement of 1662, poor people from elsewhere might be sent back to their own parish. This law was generally applied until the Poor Law Amendment Act of 1834. In July 1694, for instance, Griffin Morgan was removed to Thaxted, and it was agreed in 1740 that the overseers should obtain an order from the Justices of the Peace authorising the removal of Mary Bennett from Brentwood to Petticoat Lane in Spitalfields.

The assessment of rates, whether for poor relief or for other purposes, was liable to cause disagreement within the town. Brentwood inhabitants complained in 1655 that Thomas Danwood was refusing to pay the poor rate and to accept the apprentice allocated to him; the Justices of the Peace ordered him to pay up. Concern was expressed at Quarter Sessions when it was thought that a rate had been levied unfairly. In 1661, it was alleged that two assessments had been made, the first by the majority of the inhabitants, and the second by five townsmen only. The justices had confirmed the second rate, but an order was issued that two justices should investigate the whole matter. Quarter Sessions declared that shopkeepers and innkeepers were to be rated fairly.

The amount paid for poor relief in the early 18th century was under £100, although for a short time it increased to over £200 about 1740. The drastic rise in expenditure all over England came in the late 18th and early 19th centuries, when both population and destitution were mounting. For Brentwood, the increase in expenditure can be traced in the overseers' annual accounts, recorded in the Vestry Minutes. Some increase is apparent in the late 1780s: expenditure totalled £378 in 1788-9, and £448 in 1790-1. The trend was inexorably upwards, £753 being spent in 1796-7, £967 in 1803-4, £1,031 in 1812-13, and £1,217 in 1813-14. In some years expenditure fell, as when £575 was spent in 1825-6, but this did not alter the overall upward trend.

21   *A view of the* Gardeners' Arms, *Hart Street, taken in the 1960s.*

Many of the poor were helped in their own home, by what is known as the system of outdoor relief. In May 1697 Ann Mason's rent was to be paid as long as she continued to live outside the 'town house'. Early in 1700, it was decided that pauper children over the age of fourteen should be put out to service, and those under fourteen apprenticed; two of Ann Mason's children and two of William Wood's were apprenticed. The Vestry sanctioned payments to doctors and surgeons, and relief included hospital care if appropriate. In 1793, the Vestry agreed to remove Mary Ennever from Bethlem hospital to Mr Miles's house at Hoxton; the reference to Bedlam indicates that this was a case of mental illness. Sometimes, outdoor relief was combined with care in the workhouse. Three of Crammer's children and two of Mrs Cross's were to be taken into the workhouse in April 1797; Crammer was no longer to receive a weekly allowance, but Mrs Cross was to receive three shillings a week for herself and her other two children.

The main objection raised to the system of outdoor relief was that it was expensive and wasteful, and it was regarded as preferable to house all the poor in need of relief so that expenditure could be closely monitored by the Vestry. A 'town house' for the poor of Brentwood was mentioned in 1697, and the order to the overseer to provide wool to employ the poor in spinning and weaving probably referred to work to be done in the 'town house'. An Act of Parliament of 1722 allowed parish officials to establish workhouses and to make contracts with businessmen to maintain and employ the poor. Brentwood townspeople decided to set up a workhouse in 1737 to cater for all people receiving alms or applying for relief. Robert Maxwell senior and his wife were appointed governors and were expected to keep good order, receiving in return four shillings a week in addition to their food and lodging. The plan to relieve all the poor within the workhouse was soon abandoned, at least temporarily; in 1742 the Vestry kept a book with the names of all the poor who were to be relieved until it was decided to take them into the workhouse. To start with, a house was leased, but a workhouse was purchased in 1745, and this was probably the building in Hart Street now known as the *Gardeners' Arms*. The workhouse was extended in 1805 so that it could accommodate 60 people; a workroom and a chamber over it were to be built at the rear. The overseers and five inhabitants petitioned for further enlargement in June 1828, claiming that part of the workhouse was so dilapidated as to endanger the lives of the inmates. A plan was drawn up by Samuel Scott, and a contract drawn up with John Millington, carpenter and builder, to construct it for £255 17s. 5d. The work was completed by the end of September.

Conditions in the workhouse were closely regulated by the Vestry. When Peter Robert was admitted as Master for the year from February 1786, it was laid down that the poor were to be provided with meat, drink, clothing, fuel, laundry and mending at a cost of 2s. 6d. per head. The Vestry officers provided decent clothes for everyone on entry, the Master being responsible for clothing during the paupers' stay. The clothes reverted to the Vestry if the poor person died within a year of entry, otherwise they became the Master's property. Tea and sugar were only permitted on order of the apothecary. The work done by the poor was to be proportionate to their strength and abilities and was not to exceed ten hours a day. Any profits from their labour accrued to the Master. Two days holiday was allowed at Christmas, Easter and Pentecost, and New Year's Day was also a holiday. A payment of four shillings was allowed on the death of a pauper for washing the bedding, and of twenty shillings for every poor woman who had a baby in the workhouse for her 'better support' after childbirth. The Vestry officers were empowered to remove anyone suffering from smallpox or contagious disease, and also any persons capable of maintaining themselves.

From the late 18th century, the Vestry entered into regular contracts with local doctors for the care of paupers. In May 1797, the Vestry agreed to Thomas Richardson's offer of medical care for 12 guineas (£12 12s.) a year. He was to attend the poor of Brentwood who were lame, sick, or suffering from fractures, midwifery cases in the workhouse, and poor people passing through the town. He was not, however, to inoculate anyone unless a special allowance was made by the Vestry. When inoculation was added, the cost of medical care increased, and Samuel Butler was paid £18 a year in 1805, together with an additional three guineas for making a cure of all the children's heads in the workhouse provided that they were still cured two years later. The Vestry accepted the lowest tender from the doctors in 1812, appointing Cornelius Butler for three years at £9 a year. The cost was, however, back at £18 a year by 1815.

It was widely felt in England by the 1820s that the Poor Laws needed drastic reform. The Poor Law Amendment Act of 1834 brought in sweeping change, abolishing outdoor relief and grouping parishes into Poor Law Unions to provide help within the workhouse. The Unions were to be run by local Boards of Guardians, subject to the Poor Law Commissioners in London. The following year, Brentwood became part of the Billericay Union. The Vestry proposed in 1836 that the Billericay Board of Guardians should rent the furnished workhouse at Brentwood for £25 a year. This proposal was not taken up, and the workhouse was sold, the poor having in future to enter the new Union workhouse at Billericay. With the changes in the Poor Laws, the Vestry lost its principal local government responsibility. It continued, however, to be involved with the affairs of the hamlet until the parish council was set up in 1894, and it still meets at the present day to elect the churchwardens of the parish.

FOUR

The Age of the Coaches

The road from London to Colchester became of paramount importance to the town during the coaching age of the 18th and early 19th centuries. Contemporary descriptions of the town focus on the main road. In his *Tour through the Eastern Counties*, first published in 1724, Daniel Defoe thought that there was 'very little to be said' of Brentwood, Ingatestone and even Chelmsford, except that they were 'large thoroughfare towns', with plenty of good inns. He commented on the 'excessive multitude of carriers and passengers' on their way to London, a comment which is borne out in surviving records. London's growing population needed increasing supplies of food and manufactured goods.

More traffic meant that there was greater concern over the state of the roads. The Highways Act of 1555 made every parish responsible for its own

22 *An artist's impression of a coach passing the* White Hart.

road repair, with all parishioners providing a horse and cart if they owned them or doing four (later six) days' labour. The more prosperous parishioners were able to commute their service for a sum of money. Each parish elected its own Surveyor of the Highways to supervise the work. These arrangements were difficult to enforce, and there were serious complaints about the state of the roads. In 1622, the Justices of the Peace reported on the 'ruinous' state of the road between Chelmsford and Brentwood where deep potholes had been created by the passage of heavy waggons. The Justices pointed out that the parishes could not afford to make the necessary repairs.

About 1700 a solution was found which led to the development of turnpike roads, which levied tolls to finance road repairs. The road from London to Harwich came under the control of turnpike trusts; from 1726 the road from London to Brentwood was in the care of the Middlesex and Essex Trust, and the road from Shenfield was run by the Essex Trust. Tolls were levied every few miles, and a toll-house stood on the Brentwood to Romford road near the western end of Brentwood bypass. Parishes continued to be responsible for some of the repairs, or, alternatively, paid a sum of money to the Turnpike Trust. The standard of the main road improved greatly in the 1820s when John L. Macadam was Surveyor to the Middlesex and Essex Trust, and the roads were repaired with broken stones which were then rolled to give a smooth surface. The road was cambered to ensure that water drained away.

Coach and waggon traffic increased during the 17th and 18th centuries and journeys became speedier. In addition to the private coaches and hired post-chaises of the wealthy, stage-coaches took six passengers inside and up to ten outside. A further improvement came in 1784 with the inauguration by John Palmer of Bath of the mail coach on the route from London to Bristol. Mail coaches appeared in the eastern counties the following year, with the London to Norwich coach passing through Brentwood, and the town acting as the mail collection point for Billericay and Rochford. In addition to mail, the coaches carried passengers inside. In 1785, the Norwich mail coach, travelling via Colchester and Ipswich, left the General Post Office in London at 8p.m. and reached Norwich at 12 noon the next day; on the return journey, it left Norwich at 4p.m. and arrived in London at 8a.m. The stops at Brentwood came at 10.20p.m. and 5.27a.m. respectively. According to the *Universal British Directory* of 1793, it was possible to go from Brentwood to London and back in a day; the fare for an inside seat was 4s. 6d.

Some idea of the amount of traffic towards the end of the coaching era can be gauged from a census taken at the Shenfield toll-gate on Monday 26 February 1838. Most of the traffic was going to or returning from London, although there was a certain amount of local goods traffic with the carts of farmers and tradesmen. Of the 13 broad-wheel wagons, with their nine-inch

23 *The High Street in the later 19th century. The* Chequers *inn was on the left-hand side near the chapel, with the* Lion and Lamb *opposite. The Town Hall of 1864 and the* White Hart *can be seen further down on opposite sides of the street.*

iron tyres, six were laden with flour, mainly from the Chelmsford area, five with miscellaneous goods from Suffolk, one with wool from Chelmsford, and one with a five-ton steam-boiler from an ironworks at Coggeshall. Thirty stage-coaches passed through the toll-gate, 15 going up to London, and 15 down. Of these, six were going to and from Chelmsford, six to and from Colchester, four to and from Ipswich, and three to and from Norwich. Two coaches each were going to and from Braintree, Coggeshall, Bury St Edmunds, Sudbury and Yarmouth. The stage-coaches were not necessarily full; on average there were 12 passengers per coach on the Bury route, but only two on the single Burnham coach. Private transport passing through included five post-chaises, 26 carriages, and 22 saddle-horses. These figures give a good idea of the volume of traffic passing through Brentwood High Street. According to John Larkin (1850-1926), who grew up hearing tales of the coaching days, the coaches at Christmas time were festooned with turkeys, geese, pheasants and hares, sent to London as presents from the country. He also commented on the great wagons coming through the town, drawn by six or eight horses, or in snowy weather by ten or twelve. Some were fish vans, coming from Yarmouth, Southend and Leigh. When they were unable to proceed because of bad weather, the fish was sold on the spot.

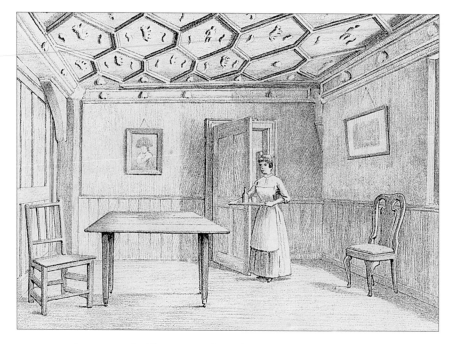

24   *A* room at the Chequers, *from the print by A.B. Bamford, 1892.*

25   *The* George and Dragon *as depicted by A.B. Bamford in 1892. This was a Wealden-type house, probably dating back to the end of the Middle Ages. It was divided into shops early in the 20th century and demolished about 1970.*

26   *The rear of the* George and Dragon *in 1892.*

The increasing traffic brought business and prosperity to the Brentwood
inns which supplied fresh horses for the coaches, food and drink for drivers
and passengers, and also accommodation. A list of inns and ale-houses for
1686 showed that Brentwood and Shenfield could supply 110 beds and
stabling for 183 horses. According to Pigot's *Directory* of 1839, the principal
inns were the *Lion and Lamb*, the *White Hart*, the *Chequers* and the *Golden
Fleece*. The *Crown* had been a coaching inn earlier, and Larkin refers to the
George and Dragon as a coaching inn. Of these, the *White Hart* was the most
important, and the excise office was located there in 1793. Larkin describes
how, as the coach drew up, ostlers had a fresh team of horses ready.
Shillingsworths of brandy, gin and rum were served, boiling hot in winter,
and then the coach was again on its way. The head waiter and chambermaid
made plenty of money in tips. The post-boys operating the post-chaises wore
uniform; a post-chaise arriving with a blue-jacketed boy was known to have
come from the *Saracen's Head* at Chelmsford, and was sent on with a fresh
team and a red-jacketed boy for the next stage. A reference to a stay at the
Crown in 1662 is found in the *Journal of William Schellinks' Travels in England*.
The landlord had a fine boxwood shove-halfpenny table, and claimed that

27 *A view of Moat House, Brook Street, taken in the 1960s. The house mainly dates from the 16th century. It is now* Marygreen Manor Hotel.

gentlemen from London and the country stayed for three, six or eight days at a time 'to gamble away their money'. The *Crown* contained the town's post office in 1793, and in 1797 was said to have had 13 post-horses and three post-chaises for private hire. By 1818, it had closed, and in 1845 was being used as a lecture room.

Judging by John Larkin's account, the inns were busy with coaches for most of the day. To take just a few examples, the 'Yarmouth Star', on the London to Norwich route and driven by Fiddler Dring, arrived in Brentwood at 9a.m. The corresponding coach, driving up to London, came in about five o'clock in the afternoon. The 'Norwich Times', operating three times a week in each direction, and driven by George Palmer, known as 'Brandy George', passed through Brentwood at 8.30a.m. on its way to Norwich, and at 5.30p.m. going up to London. The 'Norwich Phenomenon', arriving in Brentwood on its down journey at 9a.m., operated daily in each direction, as did the 'Ipswich Blue' and the coach for Bury St Edmunds, arriving at 11a.m., and the 'Wellington' which went through Brentwood at noon on its way to Colchester. The night mail coach came through Brentwood on its way up to London at 4a.m., and on its down journey at nine o'clock at night. In addition, there were daily coaches to Chelmsford, Braintree, Blackmore, Billericay, Harwich, Maldon and Southend, and every other day to Coggeshall and Burnham.

It was not only the inns which benefited from the growth of travel. Shopkeepers and businessmen were in constant touch with London. According to Larkin, shopkeepers kept a 'one-horse van and a man' to fetch their goods from London, or went to London in a gig 'with a good fast trotting nag'. Although businesses made use of locally produced goods, grocers, drapers and others needed to buy many of their goods in London.

Londoners living in the Brentwood area were able to work in the City and return home at night; others kept a base in the City in addition to their country house. The City broker William Wheatley lived at Moat House (now Marygreen Manor) in Brook Street with his wife from 1723 until about 1749. The house was bought by a London banker, Nathaniel Neal, in 1762; Nathaniel died the following year, but his widow continued to live there for another twenty years. George Morgan and his family were at Moat House between 1851 and 1882, George retaining his business in London as a wholesale stationer.

Moat House was built in the 16th century, although it has been altered and added to since. Other gentry houses in the area date from the coaching age. Among them are Gilstead Hall, known as Wealdside in the 18th century and lived in by the Wright family who were Roman Catholic bankers. The house is dated 1726 and was extended in the mid-18th century. Dytchleys, also in Coxtie

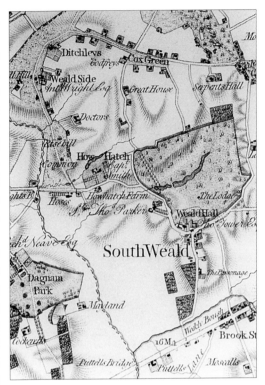

28 *South Weald, from the Chapman and André map of 1777, showing the large houses of the parish.*

29 *A view of Gilstead Hall, taken in the 1960s. The house was built in the first half of the 18th century.*

30 *Dytchleys, built in the 18th and early 19th centuries. The photograph was taken in the 1960s when the house belonged to Queen Mary College, University of London.*

Green Road, is dated three years later, 1729, and was extended in the later 18th and early 19th centuries. Rochetts in South Weald was held by Sir Thomas Parker (d.1784), Chief Baron of the Exchequer, and then passed to his daughter and her husband, Admiral Sir John Jervis, Earl St Vincent (d.1823). Both men contributed to the building. Great Ropers and Boyles Court were rebuilt in the 18th century, and Mascalls in the early nineteenth. Pilgrims Hall in Ongar Road was built between 1801 and 1804, and was for twenty years the home of Emmanuel Dios Santos, a Portuguese Roman Catholic priest who played a significant part in re-establishing Roman Catholicism in Brentwood. The number of these 18th-century houses indicate Brentwood's accessibility to the capital and its attractiveness as a healthy and pleasant place to live.

31   *Rochetts. The house dates from the late 18th century, but has been considerably altered.*

32 *A view of Pilgrims Hall, taken in the 1960s. The house was built at the beginning of the 19th century.*

By the time of Earl St Vincent's death, the coaching age was drawing near its end. The Eastern Counties Railway reached Brentwood in 1840 and Colchester in 1843. The coaches tried to keep going on routes not covered by the railway, but their revenues, and also the tolls along the turnpikes, plummeted. John Larkin relates how the railway company at first used coaches to bring passengers from Chelmsford, Braintree and Witham to Brentwood Railway Station to catch the train to London. Other coaches stopped at the *White Hart* as they had always done, and then went down Love Lane (Crown Street) to the station with their passengers for London. One of the best known stories in Brentwood's history concerns the last journey of the 'Yarmouth Star'. Going down Crown Street, the wheels of the coach grazed the fence. The horses took fright and bolted, and the coach overturned at the corner into Queens Road. The horses were unhurt, but Fiddler Dring, the coachman, broke his neck and was killed.

FIVE

Warley Camp and
Warley Barracks

Over the centuries, Brentwood became used to soldiers passing through the town. The townspeople witnessed the forces sent by Richard II to suppress the Peasants' Revolt, and armies marching to Orwell and Harwich for embarkation to France or the Low Countries, whether during the Hundred Years War of the 14th and 15th centuries, or the continental wars some three hundred years later. At the time of the Spanish Armada in 1588, Brentwood was the assembly point for soldiers from eight midland and eastern counties. The town continued to be used for mustering troops, as for the Duke of Buckingham's continental expedition of 1625 when troops assembled at Brentwood and then marched to Plymouth for embarkation, a journey which took 16 days. During the Civil War of the 1640s, Brentwood probably only witnessed armies in 1648 when the forces of Sir Charles Lucas joined forces at Brentwood with Royalists from Kent. These Cavaliers were pursued by the Roundheads, who were at Brentwood early in June and then moved on to besiege and capture Colchester.

33 *Great Warley Common, to the south of Brentwood, from the Chapman and André map of 1777.*

The establishment of the camp on Warley Common between 1778 and 1782 was very different from having soldiers pass through the town. Warley Common had been used for this purpose in 1742 and 1762, but in 1778 it formed one of a network of camps in southern and eastern England to defend the realm against the threat of French invasion and, in particular, to resist an invader

34 *The north front of Thorndon Hall, built on a new site by Robert Edward, 9th Lord Petre, between 1764 and 1770. This is where he entertained George III and Queen Charlotte in 1778.*

marching on London. During the American War of Independence, France took the side of the American colonists in 1778, followed by Spain in 1779 and Holland at the end of 1780. A map of the camp in 1778 shows that the main line of tents lay on the west side of the Common, near the road from Warley to Brentwood, with another line of tents across the Common to Hartswood. Since the camp contained about 11,000 soldiers and, in addition, wives, children and camp-followers, it was bound to have an impact on Brentwood and the surrounding villages; at the time of the first national census in 1801 Brentwood had a population of 1,007.

The soldiers came from different parts of the country, and comprised regulars and the part-time militia. Officers who belonged to the gentry and nobility were absorbed into local social life, but ordinary soldiers received poor food and harsh discipline, and many succumbed to disease. Military manoeuvres attracted large crowds of onlookers. Because of its situation and novelty, Warley camp inspired poetry, music, painting and plays, and attracted plenty of visitors from London and other parts of Essex. Londoners organised transport to the camp, such as the Warley Camp Common Stage Cart which took nine people sitting on three benches installed across the cart. For nightly celebrations, a coach left the camp for London at 5 p.m., leaving London on the return journey twelve hours later.

35   *The south front of Thorndon Hall. The portico may originally have been intended for old Thorndon Hall, which was located over a mile from the new Hall. Robert James, 8th Lord Petre, intended to remodel the old Hall, but his death in 1743 put an end to the work.*

36   *Warley barracks, built in 1805 and later.*

37 *A view of Warley barracks in the early 20th century.*

The presence of the camp brought an increase of business to the town. Brentwood chapel and Great and Little Warley churches baptised the children born in the camp and buried those who died. Because of the size of the camp, its food supplies could not be wholly supplied by the town, but there was the opportunity for enterprising men to sell vegetables and hot pies and puddings. When the camp reopened in the summer of 1779, it was estimated that there were 128 unlicensed ale, beer and liquor houses to the rear of it. Local women took in washing in order to make extra money. Inns in the High Street did good business in providing dinners and accommodation. There was a grand dinner at the *Crown* on the occasion of Lord Amherst's visit to the camp in October 1779.

The visit to the camp by George III and Queen Charlotte in 1778 marked a great highlight for Robert Edward, 9th Lord Petre, whose excitement comes through in his diary. He was the Lord Petre who built Thorndon Hall, which can still be seen from several parts of Brentwood. The large classical mansion was designed by James Paine with a central block and curving corridors to the east and west wings. As a Roman Catholic peer, Lord Petre was unable to take his seat in the House of Lords and could not play any part in public life. Some disabilities on Roman Catholics were removed by Act of Parliament in 1778, but full Roman Catholic Emancipation did not come until 1829. Lord Petre felt that it was a great privilege when the king accepted his invitation to stay at Thorndon during his visit to Warley camp. The acceptance of hospitality from a Roman Catholic peer was a landmark event not only for Lord Petre but for greater religious toleration generally.

The invitation was accepted on 22 September, with the king due to arrive on Monday 5 October. Although Thorndon Hall had only been finished eight years before, Lord Petre ordered new furniture and curtains for the drawing-room, the royal bedroom, the king's dressing-room and the queen's

38 *The Guards' Officers' Mess.*

room. New plate was purchased, and gold plate was borrowed from neighbours and friends. Great quantities of food were secured, it being a major logistical exercise to feed not only the Petre family and the royal party but also the servants and workmen. A party of French cooks arrived five days beforehand to prepare the food, but returned to London three days later when it was learned that the king would not arrive until Monday 19 October. A dinner party had to be held to consume the food which would spoil, and the cooks reappeared on 14 October.

The visit itself was a great success. Brentwood was decorated with foliage and bunting; the army lined the avenue between Brentwood and Thorndon, and a gun salute was fired in the park. The king and queen were escorted by attendants and Horse Guards, and also by Lord Petre's tenants led by his steward. They were received at the Hall by Lord and Lady Petre. On Tuesday morning, the party set out at half past ten for Warley camp, where the king reviewed the troops and watched a mock battle which was said to have been 'conducted in a very masterly manner'. John Crosier, who thus described the manoeuvres, was a farmer and miller from Maldon who had come over to see the king. In his opinion, the battle 'gave entertainment to one of the most innumerable multitudes I ever saw'. Many agreed with him that it was a grand military display. Afterwards, the king and queen returned to Thorndon for dinner, and departed on Wednesday morning to visit Earl Waldegrave at Navestock.

Warley camp was re-established in the next three summers, but by 1781 the invasion scare was virtually over. In 1780, the troops were brought into London to suppress the Gordon riots against Roman Catholics, when Lord Petre's house in Park Lane was looted and the Pembroke militia defended Thorndon Hall. The *Universal British Directory* of 1793, referring to the beautiful view from Warley Common, commented that it was noted for its 'large encampment during the late war'.

In fact 1793 saw the outbreak of the French Revolutionary War, and Warley was to become a major military centre for a large part of the 19th and first half of the 20th centuries. The threat of invasion recurred, and in 1805 116 acres of Warley Common was sold to the War Office by George Winn, who held the manors of Great and Little Warley. Permanent army barracks were built, and two troops of horse artillery were housed there. The barracks continued to be used until 1832, and then remained empty until they were purchased by the East India Company eleven years later for £15,000. The Company added to the buildings, and the chapel was erected in 1857. The Company also provided the site for Christ Church, Warley, opened in 1855, next to the barracks' married quarters on the Warley Road. The national census provides information on the number of soldiers at the barracks. In 1851, Little Warley's population totalled 988, of whom 644 were soldiers; in addition, wives and families probably numbered about 100. After the Indian Mutiny of 1857, the Crown took full control of the government of India, and the barracks were returned to the War Office in 1861.

The memories of Mark Munroe Crummie throw light on the life of a recruit at Warley barracks in the 1840s. He was born in Poplar in 1826, and on leaving school did not want a local job but something more adventurous. He enlisted as a soldier of the Flying Horse Artillery of the East India Company on 31 July 1844. After passing the medical examination and being sworn in, he and his companions were taken by train to Brentwood. They had a drink at the *Station Hotel* before marching to Warley. The Sergeant found it difficult to keep the noisy and merry party under control, but when they turned into the *Horse Artillery Man* up Warley Hill he managed to persuade the landlord,

39 *The Depot Officers' Mess of the Essex Regiment about 1914. This building is still standing.*

40 *The Essex Regiment chapel, designed by Sir Matthew Wyatt in 1857, with the campanile added one hundred years later.*

41 *The Officers' Mess of 1939. The Marillac hospital moved here after the closure of the barracks.*

a pensioner of the Bombay Foot Artillery, not to give them any more beer. On arrival at the barracks, the Sergeant-Major put Crummie into the guardroom for impertinence. The next day, the recruits were issued with clothing and 'made to appear as scarecrows'. The forage cap was as it came from the manufacturers, without lining and padding. It was blue with a red tuft on top and E.I.C. in brass letters on the front, which according to the soldiers stood for East India Convicts. The recruits had a medical examination after breakfast, had their hair cut, and were given a bath. Dinner was as good a meal as Mark Crummie said he had ever had, 'plenty of good wholesome roast beef and baked potatoes'. Parade took

42 *The Soldiers' Home, Warley Hill, about 1900. The house has been dated to about 1860, and the small building to about 1810. It is possible that the East India Company set up a soldiers' home.*

place next morning at 6.15a.m., followed by drill on the Common until eight o'clock. Then they had breakfast, which consisted of bread and coffee and 'any other extra luxury you chose to purchase from the canteen'. Fatigue parties worked during the morning cutting and transporting turf on the Common for the officers' gardens, and digging gravel for the garden walks and the Barrack Square, rolling in the gravel and pumping water. Drill parade took place after dinner at two o'clock, and the men had to fit in time to pipeclay, dry and mangle their white trousers so as to appear clean on parade.

Once the uniforms were made or altered by the tailor, the recruits were allowed out of the barracks. Mark Crummie referred to playing cricket on the Common, and drinking in the Brentwood pubs. The beerhouses at the west end of the High Street were popular with the soldiers, as were the pubs on the Warley Road. Mark wanted to be sent out to India and he left England before the end of August after enjoying a great family gathering. The troops marched from Warley to Tilbury; Mark had never walked so far before and got very thirsty and tired. They embarked at Tilbury, and during the voyage he worked in the butcher's department and was excused all military duties except for church parade. On 23 December 1844, Calcutta was in sight. Mark Crummie served in the East India Company Artillery for twenty years, rising to become a sergeant-major. He died in 1890.

43   *Christ Church, Warley, opened in 1855.*

With the army reforms of the early 1870s, the barracks became the depot of the Essex regiment from 1873 until they closed in 1959. The territorialisation of the infantry formed part of Edward Cardwell's reforms. He combined regular battalions with the militia, the old regiments carrying their battle-honours and traditions into the new organisation. At least two battalions were attached to each depot, with one remaining in England and the other on overseas service. The Essex regiment consisted of two regular battalions, the 44th and 56th Foot, and two militia battalions. The 44th was known as the East Essex Regiment from 1782, and its distinguished service included the capture of the eagle of the 62nd French infantry at the battle of Salamanca in 1812. During its service in the Boer War, Lieutenant Parsons was awarded the Victoria Cross. The 56th Foot was known as the West Essex Regiment from 1782. The militia absorbed into the Essex Regiment comprised the Essex Rifles and the West Essex Militia. Down to 1959, the Essex Regiment was a constant presence in Brentwood, notably during the First and Second World Wars.

SIX

The Coming of the Railway and the Growth of the Town

During the 19th century, Brentwood grew from a town of just over 1,000 people to one of nearly five thousand. There was a steady increase in population in the first three decades of the century, from 1,007 in 1801 to 1,642 thirty years later, and 2,362 in 1841, the year after the opening of the railway. From 1861 until the end of the century there was steady growth, from 3,093 in 1861 to 4,932 in 1901. Further expansion took place after the First World War, the population of the parish and Urban District numbering 6,853 in 1921. Although it took some time for the effects of the coming of the railway to be fully realised, its importance in the growth of the town is undoubted.

The Eastern Counties Railway brought out its prospectus for a railway line from Shoreditch to Norwich and Yarmouth in 1834, and the project was

44 *A view taken before 1934 of Brentwood and Warley station and the* Essex Arms. *The station was rebuilt in 1934 when two new railway tracks were laid through the station. The* Essex Arms *can still be seen.*

45   *The entry for the trains up to London at Brentwood and Warley station.*

accepted by Parliament two years later. The Company was then faced with litigation from landowners, eager to reap a profit from the passage of the railway across their land. William, 11th Lord Petre, received £120,000, freeing him from the debts incurred by his grandfather in building Thorndon Hall. The line from Mile End to Romford was opened with due ceremony on 18 June 1839, and the railway reached Brentwood on 1 July 1840. Delays then occurred because the running sand beyond Brentwood station made it virtually impossible to construct the essential cutting for the line. According to John Larkin, several contractors were ruined before Thomas Hill of Brentwood took on the contract, found firm ground and made a fortune. Soil from the cutting was hauled up and dumped on the south end of Shenfield Common, forming the Tips which have given much enjoyment to tobogganing children over the years. The cutting is spanned by the Seven Arch Bridge, taking the Childerditch road across the railway, and the Three Arch Bridge, taking the road to Ingrave and Tilbury.

The railway reached Colchester in 1843 and went no further as its cost had exceeded the original estimate for the whole line. Accidents occurred during the early years of the railway, as with the collision west of Brentwood in 1845. The driver ran his engine into the spare engine used to help trains up the steep incline into Brentwood. One coach jumped the tracks and many passengers were injured. Several changes have taken place since the railway was opened. Eastern Counties Railway was amalgamated into the Great Eastern Railway in 1862, and it was this company which opened Liverpool Street Station in 1874. The two tracks through Brentwood were increased to four in 1934 when the station was rebuilt. The line from Liverpool Street to Shenfield was electrified in 1949 after nationalisation.

The coming of the railway spelled the end of the coaches, but made for greater ease of movement for people, goods and mail, the contract for which was awarded to the Eastern Counties Railway in July 1843. According to White's *Directory*, Brentwood had five trains a day in 1848, increasing to 11 by 1863. For the journey to or from Shoreditch, the Eastern Counties Company charged 3s. 6d. for a first-class ticket, 2s. 6d. for second-class, and 1s. 6d. for third-class. The times of journeys varied, depending on whether the train stopped at Romford, Ilford and Stratford; the intermediate stations were built later. Many trains took about forty-five minutes, but the first up mail train to London, leaving Brentwood at 4.23a.m., completed its journey in 41 minutes, while the earliest down train (third-class only) left Shoreditch at 7.30 a.m. and took one hour and 12 minutes to reach Brentwood. The age of the commuter was still a long way off.

The railway was especially important for the transport of heavy goods, such as coal, grain and bricks. The Brentwood Gas Light Company was established at the south end of Crown Street about 1836, but it moved to new works near the railway about 1858 so that coal could be brought straight into the works. Carriers however remained in business, adapting their routes and transport to meet current needs. In 1914, Joseph Ablin ran a twice-daily service to Ingrave, Herongate and East Horndon from the *Chequers* inn in the High Street and from the railway station, while James Springett of Victoria Road operated a service to Chelmsford on Fridays which was still running over twenty years later. Carter Paterson and Company Ltd had an office in Kings Road in 1937.

46 *A view of the station before 1934.*

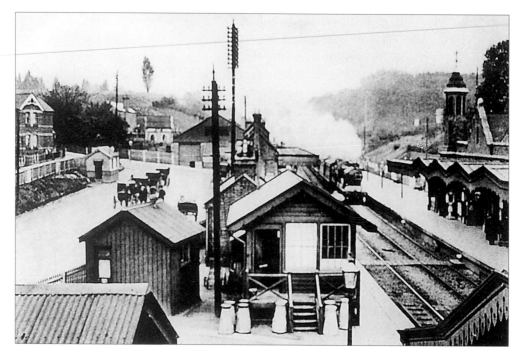

47   *The station before 1934. A train is arriving from Shenfield.*

48   *The* Seven Arches *public house, just up the hill south of Seven Arches bridge. It was demolished in 2000 and replaced by housing.*

The railway encouraged the growth of industry in the town. Brentwood was never primarily an industrial town, but brewing and brickmaking were important in the 17th and 18th centuries, and expanded in the nineteenth. The malthouse at the west end of the High Street, recorded on the 1717 map, operated throughout the 18th and 19th centuries, and there was also a malthouse in Back Street. Thomas Wright was a brewer and maltster in the High Street in the late 1820s and 1830s. Alfred Fielder's brewery in Kings Road was first recorded in 1855, and the family were also coal merchants. The brewery was taken over in 1923 and mostly demolished, but the *Brewery Tap* remains open on the corner of Kings Road and

49 *The site of Fielder's Brewery and the* Brewery Tap *on the corner of Kings Road and Primrose Hill.*

50 *An early 20th-century view of Kings Road looking up from the station. The* Railway Tavern *is on the right, and James and George H. Matthews, corn-dealers, is the second building on the left. F.W. Arnold had an outfitter's shop.*

Primrose Hill. The building contractor Thomas Hill had a brewing business in the High Street in 1863, and the business continued in the family's hands until it was purchased by Ind Coope in 1900; in 1882, it was also manufacturing mineral water, and John Hill owned the *Lion and Lamb* in the High Street and the *Railway Hotel* to the north of the station in Kings Road in the late 19th century. Their brewery was a four-storey building near the *Essex Arms*, and the malthouse was on the site of the present station car park. Edward Johnson had a small brewing business in Milton Road in the 1870s. The maltster Edward Bradley had his business in the High Street and at the station by 1870, and also at Ware in Hertfordshire. By the end of the century, the business was in the hands of John Barrett, maltster and coal merchant of Kings Road and Southminster.

A brick kiln was marked to the west of Warley Lane (Kings Road) on the Chapman and André map of 1777, and in the later 19th century there were brickfields there and in Rose Valley. These businesses had easy access to the railway. The brickmakers included the Brentwood Brick and Tile Company, and Winter Brothers. In 1855, James Winter was described as a timber merchant, brickmaker, builder and agent for General Life Assurance. His sons went into the business, and in 1905 Winter Brothers operated from Kings Road as builders' merchants, undertakers and monumental masons. Coal merchants were also near the railway. C.A. Fielder, maltster, coke, coal and salt merchant, was to be found at the railway station in 1882, as were Daldy and Company, coal and timber merchants, and maltsters, who also had businesses at Barking, Ilford, Romford, Rainham, Grays, Benfleet and Stanford-le-Hope.

51 *The factory of Ilford Ltd in Woodman Road in the 1970s. This branch of Ilford Ltd became known as Selo Ltd in the mid-1920s.*

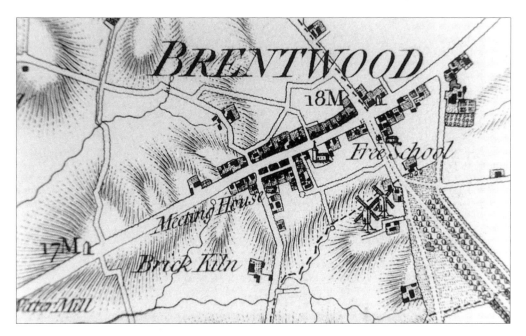

52 *Brentwood, from the Chapman and André map of 1777. The town was still concentrated along and around the High Street. The burial ground of the Congregational Meeting House in Kings Road still survives. Note the brick kiln in Kings Road, and the windmills on Shenfield Common. The avenue from Brentwood to Thorndon Hall can be seen to the southeast of the town.*

Brentwood in the 19th century was still a town serving an agricultural area, and farming needs were met by Burgess and Key's agricultural machinery and engineering works set up in 1855. The partners, William Burgess and Sir Kingsmill Grove Key, employed about 180 men in 1863. White's *Directory* for that year commented on the extensive machine works in Ongar Road, manufacturing reaping machines and other equipment. The firm continued at the Victoria Works, as they were called, into the 1920s. They were taken over by A.E. Symes Ltd, builders and civil engineers, about 1926, and closed in 1978. Thermos Ltd opened their factory in Ongar Road in 1954.

A major employer in the town for much of the 20th century was the Ilford Ltd or Selo photographic factory at Warley. In this case, the attraction was not the railway but clean air. The Britannia Works at Ilford was established in 1879, but growth of population and housing in the 1880s and 1890s, with the consequent smoke from coal fires and fumes from the gas works, ruined photographic plates. It was therefore decided to set up a new factory in Warley in 1903, and housing was provided to accommodate the workers in Britannia Road. With the development of photographic technology the factory expanded, employing 1,850 people in 1962. It closed in 1984.

53 *Shenfield Road in the early 20th century.*

54 *Queens Road about 1900.*

SEVEN

The Townspeople in the Nineteenth and Early Twentieth Centuries

Brentwood had a wide range of inhabitants and occupations, and a considerable amount is known about them through the ten-yearly national census and the trade directories. John Larkin's *Fireside Talks* and *More Fireside Talks*, published in 1906 and 1920, provide personal details of some of the townspeople, as do some of the poems of Cornelius Butler. Most is known about the people who lived in the High Street; Larkin compiled a 'Who's Who in Brentwood High Street sixty years ago', describing people about 1860, and one of Cornelius Butler's best-known poems is entitled 'The B's of Brentwood'; a large number of Brentwood surnames, he found, began with the letter B.

The gentry for the most part lived outside the town, and the 18th-century pattern of families moving into the Brentwood district continued in the 19th and 20th centuries. The best known of these families is the Willmotts. Frederick Willmott bought Warley Place in 1875, and from about 1902 until her death in 1934 it was run by his daughter Ellen, who was a famed horticulturalist and made the gardens among the best known in England. The relics of her planting can still be seen, and the site is now run by the Essex Wildlife Trust; the house has been demolished. The family was Roman Catholic and contributed to the growth of Roman Catholicism in the area; the church of Holy Cross and All Saints Warley was built in 1881, and the Willmott family financed the building of the north aisle seven years later.

Within the town were to be found professional and military families, shopkeepers and tradespeople, labourers and the poor. Many of the poorest families lived in the yards and alleyways off the High Street where living conditions were most unhealthy. Such places were Stone Yard, at the west end of the High Street going through to Back Lane, later Western Road, and Chapman's Alley, later South Street, running south to Coptfold Road. Roper's Yard was off Back Street (now Hart Street), and Moore's Place still exists although much changed. In 1841, there were large numbers of labourers and excavators working on the railway living in Stone Yard and Weald Lane. By 1851, these men had gone, and Stone Yard was inhabited mainly by labourers, hawkers and lodgers; some of the houses must have been extremely

67 *Great Stompfords farmhouse in Hart Street, as depicted by A.B. Bamford in 1892. The building dated from the 16th century.*

crowded. A few couples lived on their own, such as James Bennett, Chelsea Pensioner, and his wife, but most households had large numbers of children and lodgers. Thomas Cashirn, labourer, and his wife had with them their niece aged six, and eight lodgers, four of whom were labourers, and a married couple who were umbrella-makers. The coal carter James Fielding and his wife had four daughters and two sons, between nineteen and four years old, and also Mary Fielding, aged 75, formerly a laundress. Another James Bennett, hawker, and his wife had no children, but their 13 lodgers included a family of hawkers with two young children.

A few families were well entrenched in the town, such as the Offin family who are recorded as butchers and curriers between the late 18th and late 19th centuries. Yet, as was to be expected in a town with a rising population, many of the townspeople were incomers, often married couples who settled and brought up their children in the town. This was as true of the people living in Stone Yard in 1851 as it was of the shopkeepers and professional families. The Chelsea Pensioner was born in Braintree and James Fielding in Romford. Others came from further afield. The hawker James Bennett and his wife were born in Brighton. Several hawkers and labourers had emigrated from Ireland, probably because of the potato famine of the late 1840s. Some had come to Brentwood via the East End of London. Margaret Haggesley, hawker, was born in Ireland, but her daughters had been born in East Ham; her son-in-law came from Ongar, and she had three Irish lodgers and one from Deptford. Thomas Cashirn was born in the West Indies and his wife in Stratford. The town's population was highly mobile, just as it is today.

68 *Great Stompfords, divided into three cottages in the 1960s, before the building was demolished to make way for the Hart Street car park.*

69 *The High Street in the 1920s; by then the* White Hart *had an integrated garage. On the right, the* George and Dragon *had been divided into shops about 1906. Buses were a popular means of travel and there were several independent bus operators in the town.*

70   *A view, taken from St Thomas's church, of Ingrave Road and Wilson's Corner in the 1960s. London Transport buses had their terminus in Ingrave Road.*

Throughout the 19th and during the first half of the 20th centuries, Brentwood continued to be the centre for the surrounding villages and was serving an agricultural area. Brentwood people were familiar with farms and farming, and older residents remember Great Stompfords farmhouse which was demolished to make way for the Hart Street car park. The market had virtually come to an end in the late 18th century, but cattle fairs continued into the 1870s. In 1819, C.T. Tower tried to stop the dealers from using the fields behind the *Chequers* inn near the chapel, but the fair may well have continued there, since schoolchildren in 1870 were said to have been unable to cross the High Street to the Girls' National School because of the fairs.

With the ending of the market, the shops became even more important, with food, drink and clothing bringing in most business. In 1839, the *Post Office Directory* listed ten bakers and five confectioners (some families engaged in both trades), seven grocers and tea-dealers, seven butchers, one fishmonger and two greengrocers. There were eight boot and shoemakers, two glovers, five linen and woollen drapers, three milliners and dress and straw hat makers, one hatter and five tailors. Some businesses were geared towards agriculture,

1860, Mr and Mrs Sharman joined forces in their grocer's shop, Mr Sharman doing the serving with his wife as his assistant; 'Mr Sharman in boxer hat and white apron, quite filled up the doorway of his little shop.' Some widows and single women supported themselves by running a shop, such as Miss Thoroughgood, who had a baker's and confectioner's shop near the Ongar Road, and whose customers were mainly boys from the Grammar School. On the south side of the High Street between the *George and Dragon* and New Road, Mrs Barnard had a dressmaking shop (her husband's stone mason's yard was in Kings Road), and Mrs Newell sold bread, pies and tarts, and, according to Larkin, always had a 'huge dish of baked rice pudding' in the window.

Not all the shops were in the High Street. As Brentwood grew, shops developed in the new parts of the town. Around the railway station there was as great a variety of people and occupations as were to be found in the High Street. In 1871, James Place, off Kings Road, was mainly lived in by labourers, railway porters and maltsters, and also the manager of the Gas Works, Thomas Church and his family of nine children. Labourers, maltsters, carmen, railway porters and brick and tile makers lived in Railway Square. Labourers were to be found in Milton and Cromwell Roads, many of them working on the railway. Crescent Road had train drivers and guards, clerks, and the doctor, Newton Hanson. There were also two geologists working for the Ordnance Survey lodging in the road, and George Kirkwood, a Presbyterian military chaplain, lodged with an engine driver in Crescent Cottage.

76 *A view of Wallis's draper's shop taken in the 1970s. The building is still divided into several shops, but Cramphorn's has recently closed.*

Along Warley Road, leading up to the barracks, were a number of military families and lodgers, such as Matthew White, an army surgeon born in Ireland, and James Moody, a military chaplain who had been born in the West Indies. Lieutenant-Colonel John Eckford, of the Bengal staff corps, and his family lived in Esher House. He had been born in the East Indies and his wife in Australia. Their teenage daughters had been born in the East Indies, as had their sons aged four and two; a son aged six had been born in Scotland. They employed two servants.

The shops were situated along Kings Road, Warley Road and the Parade, and also in Crescent, Cromwell and Junction Roads. According to Kelly's *Directory* of 1905, it would be possible to meet all the household's everyday needs from the local shops. The Brentwood and District Co-operative Society Ltd was in Crescent Road, as were Edward Johnson, greengrocer, and Francis King, grocer and sub-postmaster. There were a greengrocer, baker and laundry in Cromwell Road, and in Junction Road the baker George Brown, the cabinet-maker William Davies and the pork-butcher Walter Fayers. Two hairdressers ran their businesses on the Parade. J.J. Crowe and Company Ltd, drapers, tailors and house furnishers, had a shop in Victoria Terrace, Warley Road, as well as their shop in the High Street. Also in Victoria Terrace were Thomas Cowling's coffee and dining rooms.

77 *J.H. Drake's baker's shop in the early 20th century.*

78 *Shops along Warley Road about 1910. Note the trees at the entrance to the station. W.E. Spells, 'general drapery, millinery and boot warehouse', was next to the Methodist church of 1892. The façade of the church has since been rebuilt and the towers removed.*

79 *Warley Road in 1907.*

80   *The* Horse and Groom, *on the corner of Warley Road and Mascalls Lane. The building dates from about 1900. The inn was in existence by 1770 and probably catered for those attending the horse races on Warley Common. It was known as the* Horse and Jockey *in 1778-81.*

Although the inns in the High Street were hard hit by the coming of the railway, they survived into the 20th century, and new ones were established to serve the expanding areas of the town. In addition, beerhouses were found all over Brentwood. John Larkin explained the number of small beerhouses at the west end of the town by the large numbers of soldiers coming in from Warley barracks. Before the troops of the East India Company were sent out to suppress the Indian Mutiny in 1857, they had a night on the town and got involved in drunken fights and sprees. They subsequently marched down to the railway station led by their band, and departed to the cheers of hundreds of townspeople. The soldiers also frequented the pubs along the Warley Road, such as the *Horse Artilleryman* mentioned by Mark Crummie, and the *Horse and Groom*, recalling the days of the horse races on Warley Common. Inns listed for Great Warley in 1863 included the *Prince Albert*, the *Headley Arms*, and six beerhouses. New pubs grew up round the station, such as the *Essex Arms* and the *Railway Hotel*.

The principal inns, however, continued to be sited in the High Street. Nine were listed in 1839 and 1848: the *Swan*, the *Lion and Lamb*, the *King's Head*, the *Chequers*, the *Yorkshire Grey*, the *White Hart*, the *Bell*, the *White Horse*, and the *George and Dragon*. Of the nine, the *White Hart* and the *Swan* are still in business; the *Lion and Lamb* is now the shop of W.H. Smith. The others continued to trade well into the 20th century. The *Chequers* to the east of the chapel was replaced by Montague Burton in 1939. The *George and Dragon* on

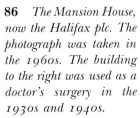

86   *The Mansion House, now the Halifax plc. The photograph was taken in the 1960s. The building to the right was used as a doctor's surgery in the 1930s and 1940s.*

stiff white cob round the countryside, for miles, to visit his patients. With his white hair and small side whiskers, rather stout, he was quite a picturesque figure … The doctor was a poet of no mean order, as some of his compositions testify.

Cornelius Butler was fully involved in local affairs. In addition to his medical work, and his work as registrar, he acted as census enumerator, and urged reform at Brentwood Grammar School. He and Dr Earle were involved in the agitation in the mid-19th century for improvements to public health.

According to the 1841 and 1861 census, Cornelius Butler was living in Cockayne House on the west corner of Kings Road with London Road, and his surgery was at the back of the house. The house was demolished in the 1960s. In 1851, the family were at the Red House, on the site of the present Marks and Spencer. One son and nine daughters were living at home in 1841, together with his assistant, John Bean, who later married his eldest daughter and went out to India in the service of the East India Company. Larkin described the Red House when Dr Growse was there. It was of red brick with posts and chains in front, and opposite the door a block of stone to facilitate mounting horses and getting in and out of vehicles – and 'for people to tumble over in the dark'.

Charles Carne Lewis lived in the Mansion House which still survives in the High Street as the Halifax plc. Like Cornelius Butler, he was much involved in public affairs. As well as being a solicitor, coroner and clerk to the Justices, he was a churchwarden and director of the Gas Company. Larkin described him as tall, thin, erect, and very well dressed, with four inches of white handkerchief protruding from his breast pocket. John Larkin saw him as the leading man of the town: 'no one ever did anything without first consulting Coroner Lewis.' He and his wife had three daughters and three sons in 1851, and the household included a governess and four servants. His eldest son followed in his footsteps as a solicitor.

87   *View of The Priory, taken from the garden. This was the home of Dr Joseph Earle. The Priory was next to the chapel and was demolished to make way for the Odeon cinema which opened in 1938. The Bay Tree Shopping Centre is now on the site.*

The name of Landon is still perpetuated in a solicitors' firm in the town. Francis Landon was practising in the town by 1839 and was clerk of the County Court in the mid-19th century. His sons also became solicitors, and Frank Landon (1854-1935) played a prominent part in the town. He and his family lived in the Red House; in 1891 he had a daughter aged seven and a son aged four, and employed a cook, parlourmaid and nursemaid. Among his public duties, he was clerk to the Governors of Brentwood School, secretary to the two Masonic lodges, clerk to the Conservators of Shenfield Common, and clerk to the trustees of the Shen Place almshouses. He was also the colonel commanding the First Volunteer Battalion, Essex Regiment. The Volunteer Drill Hall in Ongar Road was built in 1886 and sold by the Territorial Army in 1970; William Hunter Way now goes across the site. Frank Landon was Under-Sheriff of Essex between 1909 and 1910. He had a strong interest in local history, and became a director of Essex Review Ltd, resigning in 1921.

Brentwood in 1939, despite its growth, was still very much a small town with relatively little industry, and relying mainly on its shops and small businesses to provide employment and prosperity. The real growth of commuting to London came after the Second World War. The town in 1939 was a better place to live in than in 1840, and it is to the improvements in public services and community activities that we now turn.

EIGHT

Town Improvement
and Leisure

The 19th and 20th centuries saw a spate of parliamentary legislation designed to improve living conditions throughout the country, and at the same time local communities took action to ensure a better quality of life. Public improvements in Brentwood for most of the 19th century were in the hands of the Vestry and the Billericay Poor Law Union. It was only in 1894, following national legislation, that a parish council was formed, and five years later the Brentwood Urban District Council was set up, originally covering the parish of Brentwood, but extended in 1934 to cover several of the surrounding parishes. The Urban District Council of 1899 comprised 12 members, chaired by the local draper J.J. Crowe, and it met in the Town Hall on the first Wednesday of each month at 8p.m.

The Vestry was beginning to consider town improvement in the 1830s. The Lighting and Watching Act allowed it to instal town lighting if it so wished, and in 1836 a committee reported that 26 lights would be required in the High Street, with an additional seven in Back Street, Love Lane, Warley Lane, Weald Lane, and by the Grammar School. The estimated cost was £120 for the first year. The report was not immediately implemented, but a poll of ratepayers in 1841 voted by 66 votes to 40 in favour of lighting, and

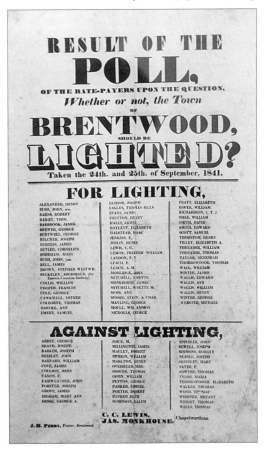

88 *The result of the ratepayers' poll in 1841 concerning the lighting of the town.*

89   *A view of the high street about 1900 with the Town Hall and its clock on the right.*

in 1844 agreed to gas lighting in the town and along the road to the station. In 1857 the lights were lit from sunset to midnight between 1 September and 1 May.

The Vestry was also instrumental in establishing the Town Hall. By 1860, the Assize House was in a bad state of repair and was demolished. The Vestry granted the site on a 99-year lease to the Town Hall Company which built the Town Hall in 1864, and from then until its demolition in 1963 it was frequently in use for meetings, dances and sometimes religious services. Its clock is a prominent feature in photographs of the High Street, and can now be seen on the Town Hall in Ingrave Road.

The real problem for the town in the 19th century centred on the water supply and public health. Drainage works carried out by the Vestry were too piecemeal to provide a real solution. The Public Health Act of 1848 set up a General Board of Health, but this could only create a local board on petition of ten per cent of the inhabitants and where the death rate was above 23 per

1,000 of the population. The agitation for better conditions in Brentwood was led by Doctors Cornelius Butler and Joseph Earle, and in 1857 44 of the 262 ratepayers petitioned the General Board for an inquiry. The report by Alfred Dickens makes depressing reading. He found that there was no regular system of drainage, and the water supply came from wells and pumps, some of the private pumps being used by neighbouring houses. However, as William Moull of the *White Hart* pointed out, his pump was so much used at night that he had occasionally to lock it up to prevent the well from being pumped dry. The number of deaths since 1850 averaged 17.7 per 1,000, but some years were particularly bad, due to poor sanitation and the 'wretched state' of many of the poorer houses. Fever was widespread, as was smallpox in 1854, and Cornelius Butler reported one death from cholera. Many of the houses drained into cesspools which often overflowed, and the open

JOINT COMMITTEE OF

Brentwood Urban District Council

AND

Billericay Rural District Council

(SOUTH WEALD AND SHENFIELD SPECIAL DRAINAGE DISTRICT).

Thursday, 24th Oct., 1912,

AT 3 O'CLOCK P.M.,

FORMAL OPENING OF

NEW SEWAGE WORKS,

Nag's Head Lane, Brook Street.

PROGRAMME OF PROCEEDINGS.

1.—Dr. J. C. Thresh, Medical Officer of Health for the County of Essex, will preside, and deliver some introductory remarks.

.—Mr. J. Edward Willcox will present to Dr. Thresh a Silver Trowel with which to place the Commemoration Stone in position.

—Mr. J. J. Crowe, Chairman of the Committee, will propose a vote of thanks to Dr. Thresh for presiding.

4.—The Company will then be conducted over the Works and the method of purification will be explained.

Wilson & Whitworth Ltd., Printers, Brentwood.

90 *The opening of the New Sewage Works in Nags Head Lane in 1912.*

drains were unhealthy and smelled very badly. Conditions seem to have been especially bad in the yards off the High Street. Stone Yard apparently had no drainage at all. The cottages were dilapidated and undrained, with great piles of rubbish in front and dirty yards at the back.

Dickens recommended the establishment of a local board of health which was to provide a full system of public and private drainage and a better water supply, and to see to the paving of courts, yards and alleys and the kerbing of footpaths. Larkin commented, 'After this, the town went on as before, only worse.' The local board of health was never established, probably because the General Board was dissolved in 1858. Brentwood received its water from the South Essex Waterworks Company by 1866, but government intervention was needed by 1871 to compel the town to carry out main drainage works, and this work had to be continued in the late 19th and 20th centuries. Modern sewerage works opened off Nags Head Lane in 1912.

91 *The County Court built in New Road about 1848. It now houses the Court House Clinic.*

92 *Brentwood Police Station in Coptfold Road, 1844-1937. Few alterations have been made to the outside of the building. It was subsequently used for the Brentwood branch of the County Library.*

93 *The arrival of Tasker's fire engine in Brentwood High Street in 1897.*

Law and order were also overhauled in the 19th century. The County Court in New Road was built about 1848. A police station was built in Coptfold Road in 1844, and was used until the present station was opened in London Road in 1937. According to the 1871 census, it housed the superintendent, William Bridges, who had been born in Ireland, one sergeant and five constables, and in the cells was Henry Higgins, a sailor from Vauxhall, who was charged with burglary. As the town grew, the number of policemen increased; John Wood, superintendent in 1926, had one inspector, three sergeants and ten constables.

John Larkin describes a riot in the High Street at the parliamentary election of 1874 when the Conservatives (the blue party) had their headquarters at the *White Hart*, and the Liberals (the yellow party) at the *Lion and Lamb*. Partisans had buckets of blue and yellow wash with which they daubed the shop-fronts and any passers-by who did not hand over beer money. The shops closed by eleven o'clock. About one o'clock a German band arrived in the town from Chelmsford and was hired by the Liberals to play in a procession down the High Street. When they got to the *White Hart*, they were charged by the blues, and the band made off to Romford as fast as they could. Fighting broke out, centred on the wide hole in front of William Carter's grocery shop on the corner of Crown Street, and many were injured. Superintendent Bridges closed all the pubs and the Riot Act was read. The town quickly quietened down, and the pubs were allowed to reopen about 10p.m. Next day, the shopkeepers presumably cleaned off all the blue and yellow wash, and the *White Hart* had to repair its windows.

At a time when people relied on open fires and candles for heating, cooking and lighting, fire was an ever-present danger. Brentwood had long had its own fire engine; in 1736, it was agreed that the chapelwarden should

94 *Outside the Fire Station in Hart Street about 1906. The fire brigade consisted of the captain and ten men, all volunteers. Elijah Andrews, captain in 1897, was a plumber.*

95 *Wilson's fire, 4 September 1909. The store was subsequently rebuilt and is now closed.*

keep the two engines in good repair. The engines, however, were not necessarily effective. John Larkin recalled the night that the *Lion and Lamb* caught fire. There was no water and no one to work the old manual fire engine, so there was nothing to be done but to stand and watch. The inn and two neighbouring shops were rebuilt about 1863. It was not until 1897 that Brentwood gained a modern appliance when J.C. Tasker of Middleton Hall offered to give the town a steam fire engine from the works of Messrs. Merryweather and Sons at Greenwich. Merryweather's agreed to provide 300 feet of the best canvas hose in exchange for the old engine, and the Council purchased twenty feet of rubber suction hose and a dividing breeching pipe. The firm took the engine as far as Stratford for delivery. On arrival at Brentwood, the band of the Essex Regiment headed the procession up the High Street, and the Brentwood engine was followed by engines from Leytonstone, Barking, Bishops Stortford and one other place. The whole town seems to have turned out to watch. From about 1902 until the Second World War, the fire station was in Hart Street, and the firefighters were volunteers. The horses for the fire engine were kept at Joseph Ablin's livery stables at the *Essex Arms*. The service became professional during the war, and moved to North Road in 1948, building its present base in 1974.

96 *Firemen ensuring that Newnum House in Shenfield Road should not catch fire. The Hunter memorial, on the right of the picture, was damaged in the fire. Local people have turned out to watch.*

97   *The day after Wilson's fire. The Tasker fire engine with local schoolboys and others.*

98 *The Convalescent Home for Children, at 55 Weald Road, opened in 1879.*

Tasker's engine came into its own on 4 September 1909, when Wilson's shop, known as the Great Eastern Stores, burnt down. The fire broke out about 6 a.m., and soon other fire engines had to be summoned, from the County Lunatic Asylum, Great Burstead, Romford Brewery and Warley barracks. The heat was so great that a wax model in the hairdresser's across the road melted. The clock continued to tell the time until 8.42 a.m., and soon afterwards the tower collapsed. There was a great danger that the houses along Shenfield Road would catch fire, but this was averted, and no lives were lost.

By the early 20th century, further changes were afoot. Electricity is first found in the town about 1902, and became available to all twenty years later. The Post Office set up a telephone exchange in 1899, and the exchange in Queens Road, built in 1932, was demolished when the automatic exchange opened in Ongar Road in 1973. The Urban District Council built its first council houses in Western Road about 1902. Local philanthropy provided for better health care. The Cottage Hospital on Shenfield Common dates from about 1883. It was rebuilt in 1895, largely as a result of the efforts of Dr J.C. Quennell, and was extended in 1921 as part of the memorial to the men who had died during the First World War. There were plans for a further extension ten years later, but Percy Bayman of Shenfield Place thought it inadequate for the growing town, and offered a 20-acre site for a new hospital in Crescent Drive. A colossal effort was made over the next three years to raise £40,000, spearheaded by Frederick Jackson who ran

99 *The Cottage Hospital on Shenfield Common, as rebuilt in 1895.*

Lush and Cooks, the laundry and dry-cleaning business. All sorts of events were staged in order to raise the money. The Whitsun Fête of 1931 raised £1,200, an ox-roasting having gained considerable publicity and drawn people in. The foundation stone was laid by the Princess Royal in May 1933. The 60 workmen were mostly local people who had previously been unemployed. The hospital took its first patients in May 1934, and was opened by Princess Helena Victoria, the granddaughter of Queen Victoria. £750 was still needed, but over £1,000 was given at the opening, and the hospital started its life free of debt. The Cottage Hospital was used as a maternity home from 1947 to 1974.

Brentwood was known for the horse races on Warley Common in the late 18th century, with meetings held over two days and prizes of £50. Opportunities for leisure activities, however, increased markedly from the later 19th century, and the importance to the town of open space was realised. Up to that time, Shenfield Common was a place where hawkers and gypsies settled and where Brentwood people dug gravel and collected firewood. Boys found it a marvellous place to let off fireworks on 5 November, according to Larkin. Prize fights and wrestling matches took place. In 1881, despite local opposition, an Act of Parliament was secured to regulate the Common, and a Board of Conservators was appointed. John Larkin approved, and himself added to Brentwood's open space, Larkin's Field and Recreation Ground in Ongar

100 *Brentwood District Hospital in Crescent Drive, opened in 1934.*

101 *A view of Shenfield Common and the Mill Pond about 1900.*

102　*The bandstand on Shenfield Common about 1900. It stood in the hollow to the south of the Mill Pond.*

Road being purchased with his bequest. King George's Field was bought by the Council in 1936 but not developed until after the Second World War.

　　Sports clubs started up in the town from the 1880s. Essex County Cricket Club was founded in 1876, and used the 'county ground' in Shenfield Road as its base for the first ten years and occasionally thereafter. Brentwood Cricket Club was established about 1881, as was Brentwood Football Club, and athletics meetings were popular. A Brentwood cycle club existed about 1891. Some of the clubs had a short life, but some, such as Brentwood Cricket Club, have continued to the present day, and more have been established. The *Brentwood Directory and Year Book* for 1922 lists numerous football and cricket clubs in Brentwood, Shenfield and the nearby villages. There were two golf clubs, the Thorndon Club, and the Little Warley Golf Club with a nine-hole course on Childerditch Common. The Brentwood Cricket Club had a large tennis section, and in addition there was the Brentwood Congregational Tennis Club and the Warley Tennis Club. Hockey clubs existed for men and women, there were three badminton clubs, and a bowls club with its green at the *Yorkshire Grey*. The open-air swimming pool in North Road opened in 1935.

103 *Sailing boats on the Mill Pond in the 1950s.*

Brentwood's Constitutional Club had its premises in the High Street in 1922, and was said to be well patronised by the gentry of the district as well as by professional men and tradesmen. It had an 'excellent reading and card room and one of the best billiard tables in the county'. Political clubs in 1914 included the Brentwood Conservative Working Men's Club, Brentwood and District Conservative Association, the Mid-Essex Conservative and Unionist Association, and the Liberal Association. The Conservative Working Men's Club met in Kings Road in 1922, and had an entrance fee of one shilling and a yearly subscription of six shillings. Its objects were listed as 'social intercourse, mutual helpfulness, mental and moral improvement, and rational recreation'. The educational element is also found elsewhere, as in the non-political Brentwood and District Mechanics' Institute, established in 1900 under the chairmanship of J.J. Crowe. The Brentwood Ladies Club had its rooms in Church House in New Road, with its own reading room and billiards.

Musical, dramatic and literary societies go back to Victorian times. Brentwood had a harmonic society between 1863 and 1890, and a vocal and instrumental society was founded in 1880. The Marlborough Dramatic Society dates from

The First Annual Report.

This Institute was founded on January 6th, 1900, for the purpose of providing a Club for young men and others of the mechanic class.

Rooms were taken at No. 6, High Street, where Chess, Cards, and Draughts were provided. Sixteen young men joined at the first meeting.

It was decided that the Institute should be non-political.

As time went on the membership increased, and it now numbers 48, with every prospect of growing larger.

A Billiard Table, quarter-size, has been purchased, and is very much used, and proves a source of revenue.

Refreshments are provided at moderate charges. Papers on various subjects have been read and discussed.

The Committee are well satisfied with the year's work, and in squaring accounts find they have a small balance on the right side.

Part II.

"Trial by Jury"

A DRAMATIC CANTATA

Written by W. S. Gilbert. Composed by the late Sir A. Sullivan.

DRAMATIS PERSONÆ.

THE LEARNED JUDGE	MR. R. T. THORNTON
THE PLAINTIFF	MISS ETHELMAY HOLBROOK
	(Pupil of Madame Eugenie Joachim, G.S.M.)
THE DEFENDANT	MR. W. H. FORD
COUNSEL FOR THE PLAINTIFF	MR. ......
USHER	MR. F. BURGESS
FOREMAN OF THE JURY	MR. GEORGE BAKER
(His original part in first performance at Brentwood, 1890.)	
ASSOCIATE	MR. F. E. D. TOWNEND
FIRST BRIDESMAID	MISS D. GADSDON
THE ATTORNEY'S ELDERLEY UGLY DAUGHTER	MISS E. A. THORPE

BRIDESMAIDS MISSES BLAXALL, W. A. BLOOMER, M. BYGRAVE, M. ELKINGTON, M. FOOKS, POWELL and G. SIMONDS.

JURY MESSRS. A. C. BLOOMER, CARTER, D. DUNCAN, HALFHIDE, LYON, F. MILLIDGE, NEALE, RENTON, SKINNER, WARMSLEY and WOOSNAM.

BARRISTERS, ATTORNEYS, PUBLIC, &c. MESDAMES ELSEY, NEALE, and H. STURSBERG. MISSES C. BAKER, CLARK, DOWSON, A. FOOKS, HOWELL, NETTLINGHAM, RANKIN, and A. THORNE, MESSRS. F. BARLOW, H. BIRD, MACFARLANE and R. P. THORNTON.

Scene.—A Court of Justice.

GOD SAVE THE KING.

104 & 105 *The first Annual Report of the Brentwood Mechanics' Institute, 1901; and a Dramatic and Musical Entertainment at the Drill Hall in Ongar Road on 24 November 1904.* My Lord in Livery *and* Trial by Jury *were performed.*

"THE WOODLAND PRINCESS"

BY LOUISE SAUNDERS.

Dramatis Personae
(In the order of their appearance).

Buttercup	Miss J. KEMP
Elderberry	Miss M. KEMP
Prince Mimblepeg	Miss T. HOWARTH
The Lord High Betrothal Maker	Mr. H. KINGSTON
Elsa	Miss H. RADFORD
Fairy	Miss V. QUENNELL
Poppy	Miss D. BENDIX
Dandelions	MASTER E. HOWARTH, MASTER R. STEPHENSON
Wild Roses	Miss M. COMBER, Miss A. DAVIES, Miss I. LEES, Miss A. STEPHENSON
Forget-me-nots	Miss MARY COMBER, Miss P. BIRD, Miss J. DAVIES, Miss M. DE GUINGAND, Miss R. FLINT, Miss T. WYNTER
Dindlebender	Master C. WATTS
Gnomes	Master H. GADSDON, Master T. ALEXANDER
Spirit of the Brook	Miss G. ALEXANDER

Scene	**A WOODLAND GLADE**

Produced under the direction of Mrs. STEPHENSON and Mrs. WATTS.
Dances arranged by Miss FLECKNOE (by kind permission of Miss POPE).
At the Piano : Miss VINCENT.

106 *A performance in aid of the Brentwood Cottage Hospital at the Town Hall on 16 January 1915. Two plays were performed,* The Woodland Princess *and* Compromising Martha, *and the Marlborough Club gave a short musical programme.*

1904, and Brentwood Operatic Society from 1906, both still in existence. By 1922, the number of these societies had increased. The Brentwood and Shenfield Shakespeare Reading Club met fortnightly, and the Brentwood Orchestral and Choral Society and the Brentwood and District Musical Society held their rehearsals weekly at the Grinstead Hall in Kings Road and the School Rooms in South Street respectively. The Brentwood Congregational Literary and Social Union was open to male and female churchgoers. A branch of the County Library opened in 1930 in Guildford Lodge, Queens Road, moving four years later to Shenfield Lodge in Ingrave Road, and in 1938 to the old police station in Coptfold Road. The Princess Royal opened the new purpose-built Brentwood Library in New Road in 1991, and the old library is now used for a children's nursery school.

107 *John Pond, a leading figure in Brentwood scouting from its early days until the 1950s. He ran the 1st Brentwood Scouts and Cubs in the 1930s and 1940s.*

It was increasingly realised in the early 20th century that clubs and activities were needed for the young. There must have been many young people in the town working away from their families who were very much on their own in their scant leisure time. The Congregational church was working with the YMCA from 1879, and their Young Men's Institute of 1891-1908 provided religious teaching, lectures, debates and sports. The YWCA had a branch in New Road by 1899, with the club open from ten o'clock in the morning until ten at night. More youth groups were founded before and after the First World War. The establishment in England of the Boys Brigade in 1883, and the Boy Scouts in 1908, followed by the Girl Guides, opened the way for groups of boys and girls to take part in a wide range of activities. By 1922, there were two Boys Brigade companies in Brentwood and Warley, five Brentwood Scout troops with a total strength of 195, and five packs of Cubs; there were Scouts and Cubs also in Shenfield and Great Warley. The Girl Guide movement started in the area in 1915, and in 1922 there were 156 Guides and 83 Brownies, with six companies in Brentwood and one each in Warley and Pilgrims Hatch.

108   *The Palace Cinema, rebuilt in 1934. The* Lion and Lamb *can be seen in the background.*

There were few societies for particular hobbies and interests in Victorian and Edwardian times, the growth of such clubs coming after 1945. An exception is the Brentwood Horticultural Society, established about 1872 and still continuing. It was considered important in the 19th century for poor people to grow at least some of their food if this were feasible. White's *Directory* of 1848 listed the Brentwood Labourers' Friend Society, established about three years earlier, which encouraged industry and good husbandry among the poor; many of the poor were said to derive great advantage from field and garden allotments.

The most popular weekly entertainment in the first half of the 20th century was the cinema. Brentwood had a cinema by 1914 when the Electric Palace opened. It was rebuilt in 1934 and closed in 1968 when Sainsbury's opened their new supermarket on the site. The Parade cinema opened near the station in 1922 but closed before the Second World War. The Odeon cinema was built on the site of The Priory in 1938, and was demolished in 1974 to make way for the Bay Tree shopping centre.

109   *The Odeon cinema. The photograph was taken just before its demolition in 1974.*

The JUBILEE OX, which was Grazed by C. M. Stanford, Esq., and which was Given by Mr. George Nicholls, of the York-shire Grey Hotel, will be Slaughtered early on Monday, 20th June, 1887, by Mr. Edwin Knightbridge (the Master Butcher), of Brent-wood, assisted by his seven Brothers :—

Mr. Henry Knightbridge, Butcher, Walthamstow.
Mr. George Knightbridge, Butcher, Brentwood.
Mr. James Knightbridge, Butcher, Romford.
Mr. Walter Knightbridge, Butcher, Woodford.
Mr. Frank Knightbridge, Butcher, Havering.
Mr. Arthur Knightbridge, Butcher, Kelvedon Hatch.
Mr. William Knightbridge, Butcher, Kelvedon Hatch.

The Furnaces, each 12 feet in length, 5 feet in height, and 4 feet 6 inches in depth, were built by Messrs. Winter Brothers, and the Spit and Roasting Apparatus were constructed (free of charge) by Messrs. W. J. & C. T. Burgess, from designs specially prepared by Mr. T. W. Haws, of Brentwood (the Master Cook).

The Fires will be Lighted on Monday, 20th June, at 9 p.m.

The Roasting will Commence about 3 a.m. on Tuesday, 21st June, and will be proceeded with under the control of the Master Cook, assisted by Mr. James White, Mr. C. O. Burley, and Mr. Walter Newman.

The Fuel will consist of Wood, Coal, and Coke. The Wood has been given by C. J. H. Tower, Esq., the Lord of the Manor; and the Coal and Coke by Messrs. Fielder and Co.

The Baster, 9 feet in length, is the gift of Mr. George Paul, and has been specially made for the occasion.

The Honble. Frederick Petre will Cut the First Slice, about 1.30 p.m., assisted by the Knightbridge Brothers.

The Meat, when Roasted, will be Distributed by Quarter-master-Sergeant Chalk (the Chief Steward), and by the following Members of the Brentwood Volunteer Company as Assistant Stewards :—

110 & 111 *Celebrations for Queen Victoria's Golden Jubilee, 1887; and a shop decorated for the coronation of Edward VII and Queen Alexandra, 1902.*

From time to time festivities involved the whole town, as when George III visited Thorndon, and when Tasker's fire engine arrived. Royal events were the occasion for major celebration. Queen Victoria's Golden Jubilee in 1887 was celebrated by the roasting of an ox given by George Nicholls of the *Yorkshire Grey* and slaughtered by the local butcher Edwin Knightbridge and his brothers. The furnaces were 12 feet long and fired by coke and coal from Messrs Fielder and Company; C.J.H. Tower provided the wood, and Messrs Burgess the roasting apparatus. Roasting began at 3a.m. on Tuesday 21 June, and the first slice was due to be carved at 1.30p.m. Bread was supplied by the local bakers. A plate of meat and bread cost 1s. 6d. and a 'thumb piece' cost 6d. Music was provided by the band of the First Volunteer Battalion of the Essex Regiment.

A full programme of events was planned for Edward VII's coronation, set for 26 June 1902. The morning was to be taken up with a coronation service at St Thomas's church, preceded by a High Street procession of the local

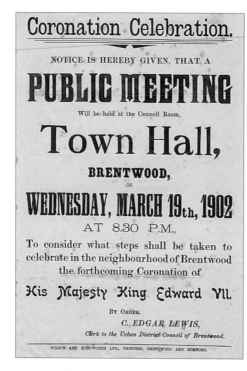

Coronation Celebration.

NOTICE IS HEREBY GIVEN, THAT A

PUBLIC MEETING

Will be held at the Council Room,

Town Hall,

BRENTWOOD,

ON

WEDNESDAY, MARCH 19th, 1902

AT 8.30 P.M.,

To consider what steps shall be taken to celebrate in the neighbourhood of Brentwood the forthcoming Coronation of

His Majesty King Edward VII.

BY ORDER.

C. EDGAR LEWIS,

Clerk to the Urban District Council of Brentwood.

WILSON AND WHITWORTH LTD., PRINTERS, BRENTWOOD AND ROMFORD.

NOTICE.

POSTPONEMENT OF THE CORONATION

Owing to the serious illness of his Majesty,

ALL THE

CORONATION FESTIVITIES

At Brentwood (excepting the Dinner to the aged Parishioners, and the Tea to the children) have been POSTPONED.

The Dinner will take place, as arranged, in the Drill Hall, at 1 o'clock, and the Children's Tea, in the Grammar School Field, at 4.30 p.m.

There being no Sports the Children will assemble at 4.30 instead of 2.30.

By order of the Committee.

HARCOURT P. LANDON, *Hon. Sec.*

N.B.—There will be a Special Intercessory Service, at the Parish Church, on Thursday Morning at 11.30.

Wilson and Whitworth Limited, Printers, Brentwood and Romford.

112 *Planning the celebrations for Edward VII's coronation, 1902.*

113 *The postponement of Edward VII's coronation owing to the king's illness.*

Friendly Societies, the Fire Brigade and the Urban District Council, led by the local Yeomanry band. A dinner for the aged inhabitants was to take place in the Drill Hall at one o'clock, followed by Sports on the 'High Land Estate' between 2.30p.m. and six o'clock, and children's Sports, Entertainment and Tea on the Grammar School field in Sawyers Hall Lane between 2.30p.m. and seven o'clock. Each child was to be given a coronation mug. The band would play on Shenfield Common in the evening, and a bonfire would be lit at ten o'clock. Unfortunately, because of the king's illness, the coronation had to be postponed, but Brentwood went ahead with the old people's dinner and the children's tea. A special service to pray for the king's recovery was held in the parish church.

As a result of the improvements of the 19th and early 20th centuries, Brentwood became a much better place to live. Basic problems of public health and security had been tackled. The establishment of the Urban District Council meant that Brentwood people gained a greater voice in local government. They had a wider range of activities than before, and technical advances meant that they came into increasing contact with the outside world through newspapers and the cinema.

NINE

Brentwood's Churches

St Thomas's chapel was a focal point for the town until the 19th century. Although it ranked as a chapel of ease within the parish of South Weald, Brentwood's inhabitants looked on it as their own church, to be maintained against any attempts at closure. It was not until 1873 that a separate parish of Brentwood was created. The growth of religious toleration meant that the 18th and still more the 19th and 20th centuries saw new churches established for other Christian groups within the town. It was only in 1689 that the Toleration Act allowed freedom of worship to Nonconformists, and still later, in 1829, that this was conceded to Roman Catholics.

114 *The chapel ruins surrounded by other buildings, taken from A.B. Bamford's print of 1892.*

St Thomas's chapel was in the care of the Vestry, and by the 1830s was too small for the growing town and in need of repair. A proposal to rebuild the chancel was rejected in 1830 in favour of thorough repairs. These, however, were not carried out, since it was decided to build a new church in a nursery garden south of the High Street on the site of the present St Thomas's church. Certain furnishings were removed from the chapel: the pulpit and reading-desk, the board with the Ten Commandments, the benefaction boards, the font, clock, bells and bell-ropes, the statue of St Thomas of Canterbury, and some stained glass depicting the royal arms and the red cross in the east window. Also moved

115   *The new St Thomas's church, built in 1835 in a nursery garden to the south of the High Street. The Girls' National School is on the left of the picture, and the Grammar School's Old Big School on the right.*

116   *The present St Thomas's church, built on the same site as the 1835 church, and consecrated in 1883.*

123 *The Baptist Chapel in 1969.*

with the Primitive Methodist chapel established early in the 20th century further up Warley Hill. The Methodists had a longstanding close association with Warley barracks, with the Methodist minister acting as chaplain to the soldiers.

There was a strict Baptist church in Brentwood in the mid-19th century, but the present Baptist church dates from about 1885. It owed its establishment to the great preacher Charles Spurgeon, who financed and sent out evangelists and saw Brentwood as a potential Baptist centre. To start with, the mission services were held in the Town Hall, but Brentwood Tabernacle was soon built in Kings Road; this was known as the 'Tin Tabernacle' and sold in 1910, services for the next five years again taking place in the Town Hall. The church had serious problems over finance and poor attendance early on. It was during the ministry of Henry Prothero Ford (1912-32), who worked for the International Tea Company, that the site of the present church on the corner of Kings Road and Kings Chase was bought for £325, and the new church opened in 1915. The building has been altered over the years, but continues to be the centre for services and other activities.

All the churches were beset by financial problems from time to time, and the bazaar combined money raising with a social occasion. The Victorian bazaar was very much in the hands of the ladies, and the stalls, as evidenced by Cornelius Butler's poems, concentrated on needlework and fancy goods: clothing for all ages, screens, purses, reticules, toys and sketches. Ye Olde Englishe Faire, held by the Primitive Methodists in 1914, had its needlework and fancy stalls, a gentlemen's stall, and stalls for flowers and fruit, sweets, books and music. There were teas and refreshments, a gypsy tent, shooting gallery, hoop-la, and a weighing machine. A phrenologist was on hand to give 'delineations of character', and ye Faire Poste and Wireless Telegraph Office

124   *The Roman Catholic church, built in 1861 on the corner of Ingrave Road and Queens Road. It is dedicated to the Sacred Heart and St Helen.*

sent 'fairygrams' by wireless to any part of the fair for 2d. for 12 words. A concert was held in the evening. As Cornelius Butler put it on another occasion,

> We have studied your tastes, kind friends one and all,
> Come buy and delight us by clearing each stall.

Sunday School was an important part of the life of all these churches, and entailed a strong commitment on the part of the teachers. Baptist Sunday School teachers in the 1920s attended morning service, took Sunday School in the afternoon, then visited absent children, returning for the prayer meeting, evening service and the Testimony meeting which ended at half past eight. Sunday School met every week, and it became usual to have a summer outing, the Congregational children going to Walton-on-the-Naze in July 1914, and the Baptists usually taking the train to Southend or Maldon in the years after the First World War; 120 joined the outing in 1922. A description survives of the Sunday School at the Congregational church in 1908 by Hedley Walter, who became Sunday School superintendent in 1936-9, and was also a deacon, lay preacher and officer of the Boys Brigade. Sunday School opened at 2.30p.m. About a hundred infants sat in long tiered rows in the smaller hall, while the older children sat in their classes in the larger hall. The afternoon began with two hymns, a prayer and a Bible reading, followed by teaching in the classes for 45 minutes. At the end, the superintendent gave a short summary of the lesson to the assembled school, read out the notices, and the proceedings ended with a hymn and a prayer. There were 440 Sunday School pupils in 1908.

Roman Catholics were present in the Brentwood area from the 16th century. The leading Roman Catholic family were the Petres of Thorndon Hall, and there were several gentry families, such as the Manbys of Bawds Hall, and the Leschers of Boyles Court. Disabilities on Roman Catholics were not fully removed until the Act for Roman Catholic Emancipation in 1829. The history of the present Roman Catholic church in Brentwood really begins with the arrival at Pilgrims Hall in 1814 of Emmanuel Dios Santos, a wealthy Portuguese priest. He built a chapel there which was licensed for public worship, and local Roman Catholics attended his services until his death in 1834. It was then decided to build a new chapel, dedicated to St Helen, on land donated by Lord Petre in Ingrave Road opposite the Grammar School. According to the religious census of 1851, 333 attended the two Masses on 30 March, many being soldiers from Warley barracks, and 80 children attended the Sunday School. It was soon apparent that the chapel was inadequate for the size of congregation, and it was replaced in 1861 by the church dedicated to the Sacred Heart and St Helen which can still be seen as part of the present cathedral. In 1917, Brentwood became the centre of a Roman Catholic diocese, and the church gained the status of a cathedral.

The original chapel became a school, run by the Convent of Mercy which came to the town in 1872. The Convent also ran boys' and girls' orphanages which included children from many parts of the world. In 1891, the Convent had 12 sisters, most of whom were engaged in teaching, but also including a laundress, housemaid and cook. The 29 female orphans came from various parts of England, and from Guernsey, India and Paris.

125 *The neo-classical Roman Catholic cathedral, built in 1989-91. The Victorian church was incorporated into the new building and can be seen in the background.*

126 *A view, taken about 1900, of Middleton Hall, the home of Countess Tasker. The house dates from the 18th century. Since 1949, it has been the Preparatory School of Brentwood School.*

Of the Roman Catholics in Brentwood in the later 19th century, Countess Tasker (1823-88) stands out. She was the daughter and only surviving child of Joseph Tasker of Middleton Hall who on his death in 1861 left her £500,000, and she was created a Countess of the Holy Roman Empire by Pope Pius IX in 1870 for her generosity in building convents, schools and churches. She contributed to the building of the Convent of Mercy, and laid the foundation stone on 19 July 1873. She endowed the boys' orphanage, and gave the money for building the church of Holy Cross and All Saints, Warley. She also financed the building of Roman Catholic churches in Ongar and Southend, and was a generous philanthropist to Roman Catholics in London. She was godmother to Ellen Willmott. At her death, Requiem Masses were held at the churches of Holy Cross, Warley, and at Holy Trinity, Brook Green in Hammersmith, and she was buried at Fulham.

There were other religious groups in the town, such as the Quakers in 1808-11, and the Salvation Army at various times in the late 19th and early 20th centuries. The Full Gospel church in Primrose Hill opened in 1928, originally meeting in the Glad Tidings Hall in Queens Road. The Evangelical Free Church in Doddinghurst Road started in Kings Road in 1953, and the Peniel Pentecostal Church dates from 1975. The second half of the 20th century has seen an increasing emphasis on ecumenical activity. The Brentwood and District Council of Churches was established in 1948, and more recently Churches Together in Brentwood has set a pattern for the 21st century.

TEN

The Town's Schools

Schooling became of increasing concern in the 19th and 20th centuries at local and national levels. Parents wanted an education for their children which would be relevant to their future needs, while national government realised that the training of the workforce was essential. Although attention originally focused mainly on primary education, the 20th century witnessed greater emphasis on secondary schooling and on the education of girls as well as boys. In looking at Brentwood's schools, the churches' involvement in education, parental concerns, and the ongoing legislative programme of central government all have to be borne in mind.

The Grammar School had been founded by Sir Antony Browne to give a free education to local boys living in parishes within three miles of the school. During the time that Charles Tower was schoolmaster between 1806 and 1825, boys could have a traditional education in the classics, or take a more general course in English, Geography, History and various branches of Mathematics, and this met the needs of boys who were going to become farmers and tradesmen. The number of pupils increased, and of the 103 boys in 1823 only three studied the classics. However, a report from the Charity Commission in 1824 stated that the school was not fulfilling its duty to provide a classical education. Numbers consequently fell drastically, and local people protested about the reversion to a purely grammar school. A public inquiry was held at the *White Hart* in 1847, and the school was reconstituted by Act of Parliament four years later; its organisation was overhauled and the curriculum broadened. Free education was only available to boys who learned Latin and Greek, however, and a fee of £4 a year had to be paid for modern subjects. The school certainly grew, and under W.D. West as headmaster (1852-70) a building programme was undertaken, including new classrooms, a swimming bath and the chapel. Cricket and football were played, Speech Day was inaugurated in 1852, and the first school play was produced eight years later. Yet local people felt that the school was only catering for the well-off.

It was under the headmasters Edwin Bean (1891-1913) and James Hough (1914-46) that the school expanded along modern lines. (Edwin Bean was the grandson of Cornelius Butler, his father having been Dr Butler's assistant

127 *Brentwood School, photographed soon after the opening of the main school building in 1910.*

before going out to India.) Edwin Bean became headmaster at a time when there had been a further decline in numbers and a loss of morale, and he probably appreciated local people's grievances. The new scheme of government of 1893 provided for scholarships to be awarded to boys from local elementary schools. The Preparatory School opened in 1892. Bean was anxious to ensure that the school was an integrated whole with high standards. Science teaching was encouraged, with the first science laboratory dating from 1893. Expansion included the purchase of the main playing field in 1904, and the building in 1910 of the main school, costing £8,155 os. 4d. Evelyn Heseltine of Great Warley was the principal benefactor, donating the site, contributing £3,600 to the building, and giving the tower and clock, sanatorium, swimming bath and changing rooms. James Hough was also a great benefactor of the school, purchasing many of the adjoining houses. The Memorial Hall was built in 1924, the chapel enlarged in the following year, the library built in 1929, and the Lawrence building in 1934. The size of the school increased from 211 pupils in 1913 to 887 in 1946. Edwin Bean had started with 40 boys.

There was some provision for elementary education in the town before the 19th century, but the information is sporadic, and it is likely that many children received no schooling. A small charity school existed in 1715 where six girls were taught to read, sew and knit. The Sunday School movement of the late 18th century provided a boost to elementary education, and children were taught reading and religious principles, and sometimes writing and arithmetic. Brentwood in 1807 had an Anglican Sunday School for about fifty boys and girls, and a Congregational Sunday School for about twenty. There were also six schools to which about eighty children went, and these were probably dames' schools for small children. In 1819, the master of Brentwood School, Charles Tower, taught poor children free for two and a half days a week, held a Sunday School for 70-80 children, and paid for a school of industry for twelve girls.

Elementary education grew under the auspices of the churches. Brentwood did not have a Congregational school, although the matter was discussed in the 1870s and 1880s when there were abortive negotiations over having Nonconformist managers at the National Schools. Brentwood had two Church of England National Schools, established in the 1830s, and attended in 1839 by 80 girls and 110 boys. The National Society for Promoting the Education of the Poor according to the Tenets of the Church of England was founded in 1811, and before Forster's Education Act of 1870 was largely responsible for elementary education in England, along with the British and Foreign School Society which catered for Nonconformists. Teaching was carried out on the Madras (or monitorial) system, under which older children taught the younger, although pupil-teachers were used once they were authorised in 1846.

The Rev. F.W. Rhodes was responsible for setting up the Girls' and Boys' National Schools in Brentwood. He applied to the National Society for the funding of a girls' school in 1834, estimating the cost at £140: £120 for a single-room brick building, £10 for the site and £10 for furnishings. The site was at the south end of Moores Place, near the 1835 church; St Thomas's Road did not exist until much later, and the school was in the nursery garden surrounding the church. The girls were taught reading, writing, arithmetic and needlework; religious instruction for boys and girls was given by the clergy. The Boys' School took over the old chapel where, apart from laying a wooden floor, few changes were made. The boys were taught reading, writing and arithmetic; an early plan to teach the older boys shoemaking and tailoring was discontinued. Finance came from subscriptions, the children's pence (abolished in 1891), and endowments; John Cotton bequeathed £100 to the schools in 1838, and John Offin, butcher, £500 to the Girls' School two years later. The Rev. William Tower, master of the Grammar School from 1825 to 1847, provided £80 a year for the Boys' School, leading to complaints that he was diverting money from the Grammar School. Finances were tight. In 1847-8, the income of the Girls' School amounted to £58 and the expenditure to £49 12s. od.; the headmistress was paid £40, repairs amounted to £2 14s. od., books and stationery to £4 13s. od., and candles and fuel to

128 *The National Schools of 1869, looking from the playground towards Coptfold Road. Coptfold House, the Brentwood centre for Essex County Council Social Services, now occupies the site.*

129 *Sports Day at St Thomas of Canterbury School, 1934.*

130 *Sports Day at St Thomas of Canterbury School, 1934.*

£2 5s. od. Both schools became overcrowded, although the situation at the Girls' School was alleviated by the opening of a separate room in Queens Road for the infants in the 1860s. Attendance was affected by bad weather and epidemics, and children were kept at home to help their parents and to work. Picking fruit, haymaking and gleaning led to absence during the summer. The Essex Agricultural Show was regarded as the occasion for a holiday.

Overcrowding and the poor state of repair of the schools led to the decision in 1869 to build new schools in Love Lane (Coptfold Road). The schools were set back from the road, with the boys' school on the east side, the girls' on the west, and the infants in the centre. They were designed for 220 girls and infants, and 130 boys from the labouring and poorer classes of the district of Brentwood. The great problem in the late 19th and early 20th centuries continued to be overcrowding, partly because of the growth of the town, and partly because education became compulsory in 1880. By 1879, there were 441 pupils, and new classrooms had to be built in 1883 and again ten years later. The infants' schoolroom became so crowded that a new school was needed well before it was built in 1914. The building programme meant that money was short, although annual government grants were received from 1871, and the Education Committee of Essex County Council took over the maintenance of the school after the

Balfour Education Act of 1902. The overcrowding was eased when Brentwood Senior Boys' and Girls' Schools (now Sawyers Hall College) opened in 1936 and all children over the age of eleven were moved there. The school then became a junior mixed school with 326 pupils. It moved to new buildings in Sawyers Hall Lane in 1968.

New primary schools reflected the growth of the town and its churches. Roman Catholic schools existed in the late 1830s and 1840s, and the school moved into the old St Helen's chapel in 1861 and received an annual government grant from 1872. The Infants' School still faces the cathedral, but the Junior School moved to Sawyers Hall Lane in 1973. A school was built alongside Christ Church in 1854-5 on a site given by the East India Company; an infants' classroom was added in 1868, and government grants were received from 1870. By then, more space was needed, and a school for 118 infants was built in Crescent Road in 1875 on land given by the Rev. Charles Belli, vicar of South Weald. The school was managed in conjunction with Christ Church School, which had to be successively enlarged and in 1911 had 250 children. Crescent Road School was bought and enlarged by the County Council in 1913 so that it would accommodate 186 children. Junction Road School was opened by Essex County Council in 1908 for 250 boys, girls and infants, and was reorganised as a junior school in 1936 when the older children moved to the Senior School.

There were several private schools for both boys and girls. James Monkhouse, schoolmaster and a leading figure in the town, ran his Academy for over twenty years in the mid-19th century. He originally came from Cumberland and married a Brentwood wife. He took boarders and day boys, and in 1851 had one resident school assistant and 18 boarders, including boys of the Offin family and several pupils from London. He was also the insurance agent for the Phoenix Fire Office. John Larkin and his brother attended the school, and Larkin describes him as a Dickensian schoolmaster. Brentwood High School for Boys had a succession of moves in the 19th century, finally settling in Rose Valley in the 1880s. In 1905, it was providing a secondary education for 66 day boys and 13 boarders. White's *Directory* of 1863 listed ten private schools, run by men and women, with several of them taking boarders. Many of these schools were small and short-lived.

One school which started as a private school continues to function in Brentwood. In 1876, Kate Bryan opened a school for girls in Fairview House, and three years later built Montpelier House, on the corner of Rose Valley and Queens Road, as a day and boarding school. There were 13 boarders in 1891, aged between seven and nineteen, coming from London, Middlesex, Surrey and Suffolk, and one British subject from Brazil. Four teachers lived in, and taught English, French, music and painting. The school also offered religious education, according to the tenets of the Church

131   *Looking up London Road to the High Street in about 1906. James Monkhouse's Academy was held in the ivy-covered house to the right in the mid-19th century.*

132   *Montpelier House, Queens Road, built by Kate Bryan as a school for girls in 1879.*

of England, Mathematics, History, Geography, Hygiene, Nature Study, Physiology, Needlework and Drill. The pupils played tennis and hockey. The school was described in 1905 as the best girls' private school in Brentwood.

The early 20th century saw growing concern over girls' secondary education. The Balfour Education Act of 1902 made Essex County Council responsible for all secondary education in the county. The County Council ran a technical school in New Road between 1910 and 1936. It was realised that a county secondary girls' school would be needed in Brentwood, and the County Council bought the present site of Brentwood County High

School in 1912, took over Montpelier House the following year, and proceeded to draw up plans for a new school. No progress could be made during the First World War and there were numerous delays in the early 1920s. By then, Montpelier House was seriously overcrowded. Classes had to be held in a variety of places, including the Grinstead Hall in Kings Road. Plans for a school of 250 pupils were drawn up in 1924, and the school opened with 204 girls three years later. Further building took place in 1936-7 to provide a three-form entry, and in September 1937 the school had 525 pupils. It catered for children aged between five and eighteen, but the sixth form was very small compared with the present day. The preparatory department closed about 1950.

The Ursuline Convent High School was established because of the number of Roman Catholic families in Brentwood. It was founded in 1900 by three Ursuline nuns from Upton in West Ham who took over Matlock in Queens Road for their convent and schools. St Philomena's day school was designed for tradesmen's daughters, and St Mary's boarding school for the nobility; Father Norris informed the nuns that the two groups could not be taught together. The two schools merged in 1919. St Philomena's taught reading, writing and arithmetic, French, music, needlework and art.

133 *Brentwood County High School, opened in 1927. The photograph was taken soon after the opening.*

134   *The Ursuline Convent and School in 1904.*

The Ursulines moved to Fairview in 1901, again in Queens Road. The schools had 52 pupils by Easter, 1902, and over seventy by 1904. By 1920, the figure had risen to 300, including 80 boarders. Expansion took place both before and after the First World War. A new teaching block and chapel were built in 1921 when the school was recognised by the Board of Education as a public secondary school. The building programme culminated in the building of Trinity wing in 1936 and a new assembly hall in 1940. A preparatory school was established by 1919.

Many of the school activities of the period before 1939 have their parallels in schools today. Brentwood County High School had its first Speech Day in 1921, school outings became more frequent from the 1920s, and a Sports Day and Sixth Form Dance were held in 1928. A party visited the League of Nations' headquarters in Geneva in 1931. The Ursuline performed its Nativity Play regularly from 1912. Although the size and organisation of the schools have changed radically since 1945, it is still possible to enter into the activities of the earlier period.

ELEVEN

Brentwood since 1939

The outbreak of the Second World War in 1939 put a temporary stop to the growth of the town, and had a greater impact on people's lives than earlier wars. The First World War affected civilian lives through conscription and Zeppelin attacks, but the Second World War involved the majority of the civilian population in one way or another, and the more intensive bombing led to greater loss of life and property. The effects of the war on a family have been graphically described by Vera Bird in *War Comes to Honeypot Lane.*

135 *The War Memorial at the junction of Shenfield Road and Middleton Hall Lane.*

136   *The Council Offices, now the Town Hall, in Ingrave Road, built in 1957 and later extended. The old Town Hall clock has been mounted on the building. The spire of St Thomas's church can be seen in the background.*

The town's nearness to London, and the presence of Warley barracks and the railway made it likely that the town would be attacked. The main road provided a link between London and the east coast, and it was thought in 1940 that a German invasion might well come from that direction. Brentwood was not on one of the four major defence lines in Essex, but the defence of the town was regarded as urgent. In the summer of 1940 concrete and steel road barriers were constructed to ring the town. Warley barracks and the Cable and Wireless radio station at Pilgrims Hatch were similarly defended. (Marconi had built their wireless receiving centre in Doddinghurst Road in 1921.) Two years later, spigot mortar anti-tank emplacements were added to the defences. Responsibility for these defences was in the hands of the Home Guard, who had their training-ground in Weald Park. Most of the defences were cleared away soon after the end of the war, but a pillbox and spigot mortar emplacement remain on the site of the radio station. Those living in Brentwood during the war would have been familiar with the road barriers at, for instance, the *Golden Fleece*, the railway station, Seven Arches and Three Arches Bridges, near Wilson's Corner, and at the junctions of the High Street and Kings Road, and Ongar and Doddinghurst Roads.

Brentwood was judged to be far enough away from London to be a safe centre for evacuees. Children over the age of eleven from Metropolitan Essex were evacuated to Brentwood in 1939, leading to considerable adaptation in the schools: 309 boys from West Ham Secondary School and 239 from Leyton County High School were taught at Brentwood School, and the mornings and afternoons were divided between Brentwood boys and the evacuees. Most boys returned home in 1940. The Ursuline took West Ham Girls School who had their lessons in the afternoons, the Brentwood girls taking the mornings. Brentwood County High School received three evacuated schools: West Ham Secondary School, Leytonstone County High School, and West Ham High School which moved on to the Ursuline. It was arranged that the Brentwood girls would attend school on Monday, Wednesday and Friday, and the evacuated schools on Tuesday, Thursday and Saturday. Normal working resumed in 1940.

Teaching staff were involved in civil defence, acting as air-raid wardens and firewatchers. During the Battle of Britain, 100 firemen who were fighting fires at Shellhaven were put up at the Ursuline which ran an all-night canteen. Local families sheltered under the assembly hall. Damage was caused by the bombing raids, the Ursuline's new Trinity wing being hit by incendiary bombs in 1940. Writing in November 1940, James Hough commented that over 1,000 bombs had fallen on the Urban District, mostly in parks, fields and gardens; however, 20 people had been killed and over 40 injured, and more than 700 houses had been damaged. Further damage was caused by the doodlebugs and rockets of 1944-5. The technical block at the Senior School was destroyed by bombs in 1944. Teachers at Brentwood County High School commented on the frequent trips to the shelters at this time and the consequent disruption of work. Over the whole war, 43 Brentwood civilians died and 394 were injured.

Once peace came in 1945, Brentwood embarked on the greatest expansion in its history. The Urban District Council continued to be in charge of local affairs until 1974. By then it had nine wards and 30 members, and new Council Offices were built in Ingrave Road in 1957. Brentwood District Council was formed in 1974 and included more of the surrounding villages, with the area divided into 18 wards and 39 councillors being elected. Brentwood became a borough in 1993, and now extends from West Horndon to Stondon Massey and Blackmore, and from Ingatestone, Hutton and Ingrave across to Navestock and Warley.

The population of Brentwood stood at 7,208 in 1931. The enlargement of the Urban District three years later raised the population to about 24,000. The figure increased by 1951 to 29,897, and to about 73,500 by 1979. The present population of the borough is 71,690. The greatest need in the years after 1945 was for housing, and the Council developed housing estates while

137   *A view of the East Ham housing estate, built in the early 1950s.*

land was also allocated for people moving out of London. The Bishops Hall Estate was compulsorily purchased in 1948, and the Council's new houses began to be occupied by the end of 1950. The East Ham estate off Ingrave Road and Hanging Hill Lane was built in the early 1950s, and when Warley barracks closed in 1959 Brentwood Council bought part of the site for houses, flats and shops. Private housing development has also been extensive, although the Green Belt has safeguarded woodland and open space. Much of the building has been infilling on existing roads, but development has also occurred on land owned by great houses and institutions. The land formerly belonging to Moat House in Brook Street was developed in the late 1960s, and the closure of Warley Hospital has led to ongoing housing development.

The development of Brentwood as a commuter town has accelerated since 1945 and the electrification of the railway in 1949 contributed to this. Changes in bus travel occurred when Eastern National took over local routes from the City Company in 1955. With the growth in ownership of the motor car, increasing numbers took to the roads. Brentwood High Street was always busy, and Brentwood bypass was badly needed by the time it opened in 1965, as was the M25 which opened in 1986. As local factories closed, notably Ilford Ltd in 1984, Brentwood people increasingly worked outside the town. In recent years, industrial and business estates have been established in Hutton and Warley, and the Ford Motor Company's establishment of its European Central Office at Warley barracks in 1964 brought new people into the town.

The expansion of Brentwood has necessitated more schooling; schools have grown, new schools have been built, and there have been major changes in organisation. Primary schools were needed on the new housing estates; the Pilgrims Hatch schools opened in 1950, and Hogarth county junior and infant schools in 1954-5. St Thomas's schools and St Helen's junior school

have moved to new buildings in Sawyers Hall Lane. This road also housed
Brentwood College of Education from 1962; it subsequently became part of
the Chelmer Institute of Higher Education and then part of Anglia Polytechnic
University until 1999. Much of the site is now being developed for housing.
The infant and junior schools in Crescent and Junction Roads were renamed
Holly Trees Primary School, and in 2003 moved to new buildings in Vaughan
Williams Way on the site of the former Warley Hospital.

New schools were also needed at secondary level, and St Martin's School
was built in Hanging Hill Lane, and Shenfield School in Alexander Lane,
Shenfield. Brentwood School became an independent public school in 1976.
New buildings have been erected, Elizabeth II opening the Queen's Building,
for science, in 1957 as part of the celebrations for the 400th anniversary.
Girls were admitted to the Sixth Form in 1965, and there is now a separate
school for girls under the age of sixteen. The greatest change in the other
secondary schools has been the growth of comprehensive education. The
Senior School, renamed Hedley Walter School after the chairman of the
governors, was the first to be enlarged and reorganised as a comprehensive
in 1968, while the County High School became a mixed comprehensive four
years later. Although there was concern in the early 1980s over falling school
rolls, and talk of closing two secondary schools, all the schools are still
functioning in 2003. Hedley Walter became a specialist school in science and
technology in 2003 and has been renamed Sawyers Hall College.

138 *Ford's Central Office, built in 1964 on the site of Warley barracks.*

139   *Members of the Historical Society visiting Coggeshall Abbey on 12 July 1952.*

140   *Members of the Historical Society celebrating the Society's 60th anniversary at Cavendish in Suffolk on 23 June 2001.*

141   *The Boxing Day meet of the Essex Hunt at the Lion Gates, one of the entries into Thorndon Park, in the 1950s.*

Celebrations and leisure activities for all ages have burgeoned in the post-war period. Inevitably there have been changes from pre-war days. In 1965, it was felt that the time had come for professional football in the town, and Brentwood Town Football Club succeeded the amateur Brentwood and Warley Football Club. The club played at The Hive in Ongar Road, but was short-lived. Other sports clubs have been more fortunate, such as the Brentwood Hardcourt Tennis Club which moved from its courts in Mount Crescent to Warley. Sports clubs in 1973-5 included cricket, tennis, cycling, rugby football, hockey, bowls, golf and swimming, and the Council ran an 18-hole municipal golf course at King George's Playing Fields. Brentwood Centre opened as a leisure complex in 1988. Youth organisations have continued to be given a high priority; in addition to church and school groups, the *Brentwood Official Guide* listed the Scouts, Girl Guides, Boys and Girls Brigades, St John

142 *Thorndon Country Park.*

Ambulance, army cadets, the air training corps, sea cadets and the Brentwood drum corps. One of the greatest changes since 1945 has been the growth of societies following a particular interest or hobby, such as the Photographic Society, Historical Society, and Gramophone Society (now the Recorded Music Society). Brentwood Museum, run by the Museum Society, opened in Lorne Road in June 1989. Together with the town's musical and dramatic societies, these have added greatly to the cultural life of the town. Altogether, there were about forty sports' clubs and over eighty cultural and recreational societies in the town in 1979.

Brentwood has continued to enjoy its carnivals and celebrations. For the coronation of Queen Elizabeth II in 1953 there were festivities all over the Urban District. The celebrations started with a concert of recorded British music given by the Gramophone Society at Norrish's café in the High Street on Wednesday 27 May. Sports were held at Rotary Hoes Ltd in West Horndon on the Saturday, and the Civic Service took place at St Thomas's church on Sunday. On the Monday, Hutton held its celebrations at Hutton Residential School, and the evening saw the opening of Coronation Cottages on the corner of Middleton Hall and Priests Lanes, Pontifical High Mass at the cathedral, and a dance organised by Brentwood Hard Court Club. The coronation itself took place on Tuesday 2 June, and the Carnival, organised by the Pilgrims Hatch Residents' Association, took place in the evening, culminating in a grand fireworks display and the lighting of a bonfire as part of the national chain of beacons. There were also Coronation day celebrations in the villages. In the days that followed, a concert was held in the Memorial Hall of Brentwood School, and a dinner and entertainment were given for the old people. The Boy Scouts, Girl Guides and Boys Brigade held their Coronation Rally at the football ground in Burland Road on Saturday 13 June.

Brentwood started in a woodland clearing and much of the woodland surrounding the town has been opened to public access in the years since 1945. Weald Park was taken over by the War Department during the war for Home Guard and military training. By 1945, Weald Hall was in a poor state of repair, and Christopher Tower sold the estate in 1946. The contents of the Hall were sold, and the Hall demolished. Essex County Council purchased the park in 1953 and opened it to the public as Weald Country Park. Thorndon Hall, where the 9th Lord Petre entertained George III, was partially destroyed by fire in 1878; the estate was sold after the First World War, and the Petre family made their home at Ingatestone. Thorndon Park Golf Club made use

143   *The east end of the High Street in the later 1950s. The Arcade, with Jacques Vinall's shop on the corner of St Thomas's Road opposite the Post Office, was built in 1954 when Rippon's showroom and garage were demolished.*

of the east wing of the mansion, and the park to the south of the Hall. Essex County Council began to purchase the park from a development company in 1939 and continued to do so after the war. Thorndon was designated a Country Park in 1971, and now forms part of Thames Chase. During the late 1970s, the mansion was repaired and converted into flats.

The High Street underwent major changes in the 1960s and 1970s. All except one of the large private houses, inhabited by doctors and solicitors one hundred years before, have been demolished. The survivor is the Mansion House, now the Halifax, where Charles Carne Lewis brought up his family. The Priory and the Red House were demolished before the war, but the process speeded up afterwards. Rippon's garage was replaced by the Arcade in 1954, and a landmark was lost when the Town Hall was demolished in 1963. Several of the old inns have disappeared, the *Yorkshire Grey* in 1961, and the *George and Dragon* and *King's Head* about 1970. Both the High Street cinemas closed and were demolished, the Palace in 1967 and the Odeon in 1973. Although a cinema was incorporated in the Chapel High Shopping Centre, this is now closed.

144   *The Fine Fare supermarket, next to the Post Office, in the 1960s.*

145 *Entry to the Chapel High Shopping Centre, built in 1973. The chapel ruins are in the foreground on the left.*

As always in the history of the High Street, businesses have come and gone. Wilsons Store closed in 1978, Woolworths in 1983, and Bon Marche in 1985, to be replaced by Cooper's Furniture Store (closed in 2003), Marks and Spencer, and McDonalds. The move towards multiple stores in the High Street intensified after 1945. The changing trend was apparent in the *Brentwood Directory* of 1969. Family businesses still existed, such as Alec Henderson, cycle dealer; S. Goodchild Ltd, radio engineers; and Cullis and Son Ltd in Ongar Road, for prams, baby wear, toys and games. At the same time, two supermarkets had been established in the High Street, Fine Fare and Tesco, while J. Sainsbury had just opened a new supermarket on the site of the Palace Cinema. Since 1969, the emphasis on financial services has led to several building societies opening their own premises on the High Street. New technology has led to shops for computers and mobile phones, travel agents have increased in number, and charity shops have been a recent phenomenon. The building of the Chapel High shopping centre in 1973 increased the number of retail outlets. As a result of a local competition, it was renamed the Bay Tree Centre in 2003 and is due to be refurbished. The most recent development has been the opening of Sainsbury's Superstore on the site of the Thermos factory in Ongar Road.

For much of Brentwood's history, St Thomas's chapel was at the centre of town life. The Becket Festival Year, 1970, saw the celebration of the eighth centenary of the saint's death. Commemorative events were organised by the churches of Brentwood, under the direction of the Urban District Council. Brentwood took part in the national pilgrimage to Canterbury on Saturday 13 June. A Sung Eucharist took place at noon in Canterbury cathedral, with visits in the afternoon to the site of the martyrdom, St Thomas's first burial place, and the site of his shrine. Brentwood had its own pilgrimage to the City of London, to the site of St Thomas's birthplace (now the Mercers' Hall in

146 *Sainsbury's Superstore, built to the north of the High Street on the site of the Thermos factory which closed in 1996.*

Cheapside), and to the church of St Mary-le-Bow where he was probably baptised. Other events included an ecumenical service in the chapel ruins on 12 July, a Becket Fair held at the new Junior School in Sawyers Hall Lane, and the performance of T.S. Eliot's *Murder in the Cathedral* in St Thomas's church. Brentwood Carnival on 25 July included a Becket float in the procession.

Looking back at Brentwood's history, certain events stand out. The establishment of the chapel and the market laid the foundation for the town's development, and its prosperity was enhanced by its position on the London to Colchester road. The founding of the Grammar School and the saving of the chapel in the 16th century contributed to its reputation. The coming of the railway eventually led to Brentwood's major expansion as a commuting town. Throughout its history, many of its inhabitants have come into the town from elsewhere, and this trend has increased since 1945. Brentwood has always been aware of the outside world. This is typified by the recent town-twinning arrangements. Brentwood twinned with Landkreis Roth in Bavaria in 1978, with the first official visits taking place the following year. By 1995, the town was also twinned with Brentwood, Tennessee, and Montbazon in France. At the outset of the 21st century, Brentwood retains an awareness of its past while embracing new developments.

Further Reading

Many books and articles have been written about Brentwood's history and those listed below represent only a selection. In addition, five books of postcards and photographs have been published which provide a wide selection of the visual evidence of the town's past and of the history of the surrounding places.

Doreen M. Acton, *A History of Brentwood Baptist Church* (Brentwood, 1884)

M. Beale, 'A hymn book dispute', *Essex Journal* 25 (1990), pp. 42-4

P. Billett, *Brentwood Methodist Church. Centenary 1892-1992*

V.B. Bird, *War Came to Honeypot Lane* (Wrexham, 2000)

J. Booker, *Essex and the Industrial Revolution* (Essex Record Office Publications 66, Chelmsford, 1974)

Cornelius Butler, *Ingrebourne and Other Poems* (London, 1884)

John Copeland and Nick Harris, *Brentwood* (Bath, 1994)

J.B. Dockery, *They that Build. The Life of Mother Clare of Brentwood* (London, 1963)

T. Jon Ellis, *Bishops Hall and Estate, Pilgrims Hatch, Brentwood. Origin and Residents to the 1950s* (Brentwood, 1998)

J. Fryer, *Brentwood. A Concise Pictorial History* (Brentwood, 2001)

P. Gilman, 'The Golden Fleece, Brook Street, South Weald', *Essex Archaeology and History* 22 (1991), pp. 76-86

S. Godbold, 'The site of the medieval hospital at Brook Street', *Essex Archaeology and History* 21 (1990), pp. 151-4

R.J. Hercock and G.A. Jones, *Silver by the Ton. A History of Ilford Limited 1879-1979* (London, 1979)

Sylvia Kent, *Brentwood Voices* (Stroud, 2001)

K. Langford, 'Arthur Henry Brown – a biographical sketch', *Essex Journal* 34 (1999), pp. 5-6

John W. Larkin (P.C.R. Linnecar ed.), *Fireside Talks about Brentwood 1906*, and *More Fireside Talks 1920* (Brentwood, 1989)

A. Le Lievre, *Miss Willmott of Warley Place. Her Life and her Gardens* (London, 1980)

Lesley Lewis, *The Private Life of a Country House* (Newton Abbot, 1980)

R.R. Lewis, *The History of Brentwood School* (Brentwood, 1981)

R.R. Lewis, *William Hunter* (Brentwood, 1955)

G. Lloyd, *The Place at Brook Street. A History of Marygreen Manor Hotel* (Brentwood, 1997)

B. Lynch, *Brentwood District Hospital 1934-1984. 'The Finished Stairway'*

John Marriage, *Bygone Brentwood* (Chichester, 1990)

K. Marshall, I.G. Robertson and J.C. Ward, *Old Thorndon Hall* (Essex Record Office Publications 61, Chelmsford, 1972)

A.S. Mason, 'Summer camps for soldiers 1778-82', *Essex Journal* 33 (1998), pp. 39-45

Peter McCaul, *St Helen's Parish Brentwood 1837-1987* (Brentwood, 1987)

M.G. McKerness, *Brentwood County High School 1913-63* (Brentwood, 1964)

M. Medlycott, *Origins of Brentwood* (Essex County Council Planning Department, 1998)

M. Medlycott, O. Bedwin and S. Godbold, 'South Weald Camp – a probable late Iron Age hill fort: excavations 1990', *Essex Archaeology and History* 26 (1995), pp. 53-64

G.S. Nightingale, *Warley Hospital Brentwood. The First Hundred Years 1853-1953* (Brentwood, 1969)

I.P. Peaty, *Essex Brewers and the Malting and Hop Industries of the County* (Brewery History Society, 1992)

W.F. Quin, *Brentwood Congregational Church. A Brief History 1672-1972* (Brentwood, 1972)

A. Radford, *Brentwood County High School 1964-2001* (Brentwood, 2002)

J.H. Round, 'The making of Brentwood', *Transactions of the Essex Archaeological Society*, new series, 17 (1926), pp. 69-74

Richard Tames, *Brentwood Past* (London, 2002)

The Victoria History of the County of Essex, ed. W.R. Powell, volume 3, *Roman Essex* (Oxford, 1963); volume 7, for Great and Little Warley (Oxford, 1978); volume 8, for South Weald and Brentwood (Oxford, 1983)

G.A. Ward, *A History of South Weald and Brentwood* (Brentwood, 1961)

G.A. Ward, *Victorian and Edwardian Brentwood* (Brentwood, 1980)

G.A. Ward, 'Recollections of an old soldier of John Company', *Essex Review* 55 (1946), pp. 141-6

G.A. Ward, 'A Brentwood surgeon: Cornelius Butler F.R.C.S. 1789-1871', *Essex Journal* 2 (1967), pp. 12-18

J.G.S. Ward, *A History of the St Thomas of Canterbury Church of England Schools* (Brentwood, 1967)

F. Whitelock, compiler, *Brentwood Methodist Church. Centenary Portrait. One Hundred Years at Warley Hill 1878-1978*

W. Wilford, 'The Rev. Charles Belli and South Weald', *Essex Journal* 21 (1986), pp. 9-12

B. Williamson ed., *Dear Mother. Great War Letters of a Bristol Soldier* (Bristol, 2003)

Index

References which relate to illustrations only are given in **bold**.
Street names are given in their modern form.